This Book Belongs To:

_____

I Started Reading This Book On:

_____

I Finished Reading This Book On:

_____

This Book Is A Part Of The Trilogy Series:

THE POWER OF TRULY HAVING FINANCIAL FREEDOM

This Book Considers:

THE TRUTH ABOUT WHAT IT MEANS TO BE WEALTHY

With:

STEPS TO HELP YOU BECOME TRULY WEALTHY

This Book Is One Of Fifteen Books From:

THE LEGACY JOURNAL COLLECTION

A Collection Of Books About:

HOW TO BECOME TRULY SUCCESSFUL

The complete collection-set entails five different series with three volumes in each series. The various genre topics experienced and portrayed in each series are completely different from one series to another and run the gamut from the spectrum of trivial to breath-taking.

The topics, experiences and personal story-lines, including myriad of questions, decisions and concluding results found in each volume are based on true stories the author has actually gone through. Raw emotion, genuine passion, sincere hopes and aspirations are felt throughout each book, which draws the reader to contemplate his or her own similar experiences and decisions he or she has made in the past, as well as seriously contemplating doing in the future.

I hope you will find insight, inspiration and direction to your life as you journey with me in this book. I hope you will be able to take ownership of this book in profound and important ways, just as I have. I truly do hope you enjoy your journey.

It's time to get to work, so here goes. <u>To begin, the first thing I want you to do is to take a look at the visual image found on the front cover of this book.</u>

- **What comes to your mind as you look at this majestic picture?**

Just as this majestic mountain scene depicts, I hope your labors in life grow and rise to great heights with horizons of panoramic vistas of great successes reached, as you strive to work hard at whatever you do throughout your life. I hope, just as the picture on the front cover of this book depicts greatness, beauty and awe, in its own right, that you too, know and/or come to know, just how majestic you truly are and how important you really are.

Also By _C. W. WEST_

How To Become <> TRULY – Rich

How To Become <> TRULY – Wealthy

How To Become A <> TRULY – Rich Kid

What Does It Mean To <> TRULY – Learn

What Does It Mean To <> TRULY – Believe

What Does It Mean To <> TRULY – Have Faith

Attitude <> Just For – Adults

Attitude <> Just For – Teenagers

Attitude <> Just For – Kids

Gratitude <> Just For – Adults

Gratitude <> Just For – Teenagers

Gratitude <> Just For – Kids

The Power Of Reflection <> The Contemplative – Epilogue

The Power Of Questions <> The Complete – Questions

The Power Of Writing <> The Continuation Of – Life

The Secret Code <> The Treasure Chest Game – Guide-Book

The Secret Code <> The Treasure Chest Game – Answer-Key

This book is the proprietary work of Charles W. West. Any unauthorized use of this book in relation to reproduction in whole or in part in any form or used for goods and/or services (including training programs, classes, workshops, seminars, etc.) is prohibited without the express written permission of the author.

All Rights Reserved by:	Charles W. West
Copyright © 2009 by:	Charles W. West
Publication by:	Charles W. West
First publication edition:	2009
Printed in the:	U.S.A.

- This book is intended for readers in both the United States of America and for International use.

- Enjoy interacting with the author by experiencing, learning and finding yourself through reading the author's many books.

- The books are from the author's personal journals, which are a compilation of his experiences, insights, concerns and directions in his life and are referred to as:

    o   The Legacy Journal Collection <> How To Become Truly Successful

    ➢ More commonly referred to as:

    <<<   THE JOURNAL   >>>

    By: C.W. WEST

This book is dedicated to my wonderful wife

This book was first written as a personal Christmas gift from Chuck to each of his children. It is a summary of Chuck's compilation of journal notes and personal experiences dealing with the topics found within this book.

TABLE OF CONTENTS

Preface:

    How To Use This Book

Chapter:

1   What Does It Mean To Become Wealthy?

2   What Do You Do Once You Are Wealthy?

3   What Has Wealth Done To The Human Race?

4   How Can A Truly Wealthy Person Be A Leader?

5   How Does A Truly Wealthy Person Create Sustainable Synergy?

6   Charity, Is It In You?

7   What Else Do You Care About?

8   How Do You Set-up Your Own Non-Profit Charity Organization?

9   Can You Make A Difference In Politics?

10   Do You Need A Break?

11   Why Should You Set-up Your Own Private Lending Company?

12   How Do You Set-up Your Own Private Lending Company?

13   Why Should You Set-up Own Micro Lending Company?

14   How Do You Manage Your Wealth?

15   Why Should The Truly Wealthy Protect Themselves?

16   Why Do You Want To Be Wealthy?

17   Why Do You Want To Be Truly Wealthy?

18   What's It Take To Put A Legacy Game Plan Together?

19   What Might Be Some Obstacles To Watch Out For In Building Your Legacy?

Appendix:

A. Complete List of Comprehensive Questions For Each Chapter In This Book:

B. Other Books The Author Recommends You Read On Becoming Truly Wealthy Matters:

C. What The Author Wants You To Get Out Of This Book:

D. How The Other Wants You To Read This Book:

E. The Reason Why The Author Wrote This Book:

F. The Complete List Of Books Written By The Author:

G. About The Author:

H. Author's Disclaimer:

Preface

MONEY MATTERS

HOW TO USE THIS BOOK

HOW TO MAKE MONEY & WHAT TO DO WITH IT ONCE YOU HAVE IT!

$$$$$$$$$

Do you want to know what I think about money? You may be a little surprised with what I have to say about it. Let me simply put it this way. There is more to money than just what meets the eye.

You will find that each book in the series, The Power Of Truly Having Financial Freedom, each has a different or unique perspective or approach to money, both in how you make money and what you do with it, once you have money. The focus of this particular book is on making money and why.

At the same time as you read this book about me and my many experiences and insights on the topic of money, you too, will come to better appreciate and understand what it is you want to do with money and what you want to stand for in relationship to money and its impact on you and all that is around you. It's what you decide to do with such knowledge and know-how and what you do with it and how to apply it that makes all the difference in moving forward in your life.

By taking the time to go through this book/journal experience your financial potential can become greatly enhanced. With such enlightenment, can bring new insightfulness of changes to make, in managing all of your financial affairs in life

This book is also intended to be used as a reflection board, over time, where you can look back at yourself in contemplation, assessment, evaluation and future decision making. Whatever you decide to do with this book as your personal journal, do it well, by writing your heart out.

Take time to reread this book over and over as you go through your life as you compare and contemplate where you are at in life with your financial affairs and what you further want to do, overcome and/or become in reflecting and further defining your financial plan of action. Each time you write in this book, either your feelings and/or experiences or in answering the many and varied questions provided herein, write the date in the left-hand margin each time you are writing those many and varied things down. If and when you may run out of space to write further, I have tried to leave extra space at the end of each chapter to continue to write on whatever financial matters there may be. When you do this, to continue writing, you need to indicate what page your thoughts and experiences are connected to, both at the origination spot and where your continuations are found and vice versa, which will act as reference points to each other in all cases. When such situations arise write the page numbers in the left-hand margin along with the dates of entry. Also, use this extra space to add more questions, concerns and things to consider than what I have provided, as such insights, concerns and questions come to you, to go in refining and defining your feelings and plan of action in further personalizing this book into your very own personal journal. Who knows, maybe someday someone will read what you write and be inspired. At least that is, in part, the hope of this book's intention.

    Now, enjoy the ride as you move forward in this book just for you. May you be a better person for the effort as you go through this book. My hope is that you will make this book your very own personal journal as you talk about your journey in life with your work, employment, business, financial and money experiences in identifying who you are and why do what you do and how to go about how to get there. Most importantly, enjoy refining and defining your money matters and financial affairs.

**THIS SPACE IS FOR YOUR
FURTHER JOURNAL NOTES ON THE PREFACE:**

Chapter 1

WHAT DOES IT MEAN TO BE WEALTHY?

WEALTHY MAN'S CHOICE

DOES IT REALLY MATTER IF YOU ARE WEALTHY?

$$$$$$$$$

- What do you want to do, be and become in life?

- How do you plan to go about or achieve becoming, doing and being what you want to be, do and become in life?

- Does it really matter what you do, be and become in life? Yes or No Why?

- Does it really matter if you are wealthy, rich or poor? Yes or No Why?

- Do you want to be poor or in other words in debt? Yes or No Why?

- Do you want to be out of debt or in other words rich to where you are free and independent from anyone or anything having any control or say over you? Yes or No Why?

- Are you out for wealth and riches of things and fame? Yes or No Why?

- Are you out to be free and independent to come and go as you please?
  Yes or No Why?

  o The wealthy and rich can choose to do what they want to do and come and go pretty much as they please.

- How can you get more if you are giving your wealth and riches away?

  o To stay wealthy and rich you must give back in order to gain more and become more.

If you want to be <u>wealthy</u> and/or <u>truly rich</u>, it really <u>has nothing to do with money</u> and things.

To be wealthy and/or <u>truly rich</u> has to do with:

1. **Being free!!!!!!!**   <>   Not under someone else's control.

    - To be free is the opportunity to do something worthwhile or in essence, to do good in your life, not to sit around and do nothing.

        o What else would you want to be free for?

        o Are you meant to be free to do nothing with yourself or to be counter-productive or worthless in life? Yes or No Why?

2. **Being independent!!!!!!!**   <>   To be able to take care of yourself.

    - To be independent is to be able to make your own choices.

    - Independence is the ability to choose how and where you might best fit into society. You can choose where you would be most worthwhile and do the most good, not only for you, but all who are affected by your very presence in their lives.

3. What's the <u>vehicle</u> that makes it possible to be **truly free?** <> MONEY!!!

    - Money wasn't intended to be just a luxury tool. It was intended to be a means of efficient commerce in trade.

        o Yes, money can buy luxuries, but it wasn't meant to become the symbol of luxury.

    - To be wealthy you need to be serious about money and money matters.

        o If a wealthy person is not serious about money and money management, their chances of staying wealthy will come and go, depending on the choices he or she makes.

    - To be wealthy you already have money saved for what you want to buy.

        o To be wealthy you have plenty of money on hand (and not just to spend.)

        o To be wealthy you want to be able to live off of your interest in the money you've saved, not just the principle itself.

    - To be wealthy you only buy what you can pay for.

        o To be wealthy you don't buy on credit and then pay the minimum payments.

    - To be wealthy you are prepared in advance, both financially and materially, to take care of yourself and those you are responsible for in any emergency, be it short-term or long-term care.

4. To be wealthy you are **living by correct principles that govern your life** and in turn govern your financial decisions.

    - A wealthy person tends to work with other people that have the same kind of goals.

    - To be wealthy is what most people think of when they think of being rich, but that's not the case. To be wealthy or truly rich is really to be far away from the fence of debt. It is to be able to live comfortably while paying for the basic things in life and being able to build your wealth at the same time.

    - To be wealthy and/or truly rich is to not have to think about how much something costs if you need it. If you want something you just get it, because you've saved for it.

Being wealthy isn't about doing whatever you want to or just doing nothing. It's about being able to do far more than just stuff for you. It's the ability to be able to care about other people and to be able to share your life with other people. Being wealthy is about having the time to help out, to care for and to make a difference in the lives of people potentially throughout the world.

There are people that may be referred to as being wealthy, but they are still stuck on their personal things or what they want to do next for themselves. In other words, they don't own their things; their things own them. It's about things, things, things. Such wealthy people are not truly free and independent. Such wealthy people may have all of the money in the world, but they aren't any better off than a poor person. They are still being controlled by someone or something else.

If you want to be wealthy, then don't be selfish when you truly do have freedom and independent riches of your very own. By being wealthy, you are on the road to becoming truly wealthy. Use money wisely and you will always be truly wealthy. A truly wealthy person asks the question why, not because he or she is trying to get out of doing something, but because he or she wants to understand the situation better, in order to come up with the best solutions possible.

A **truly** <u>wealthy person</u> **wants to help other people.** They want to share what they have. They want to help other people be successful too. It's a part of who they are. It gives added value to being truly wealthy. It is what being truly wealthy is all about. A truly wealthy person puts other people first.

- What's your choice going to be?

- If you don't want to be truly wealthy, then stop reading.

- If you want to be truly wealthy, then read on.

Remember, you can't solve all of the world's problems, but you sure can make a difference.

Being truly wealthy is making a difference in the lives of other people around you.

Being truly wealthy means that you have the time and the means to make a difference in the world and you are doing it.

$$$$$$

**THIS SPACE IS FOR YOUR
FURTHER JOURNAL NOTES ON CHAPTER 1:**

Chapter 2

WHAT DO YOU DO ONCE YOU ARE WEALTHY?

BECOME TRULY WEALTHY

LEARN HOW TO SHARE!!!

$$$$$$$$$

- What does it mean to be wealthy?

    o The beginning of being wealthy is the end result of becoming truly rich or in other words out of debt.

    o The end result of being really wealthy is to be so far from debt that it will never happen to you in your lifetime and possibly not in your posterity's lifetime either.

- What does it mean to be truly wealthy?

    o Being truly wealthy has nothing to do with making money.

    o Being truly wealthy has to do with what you do with your money.

Here are some examples of how to be truly wealthy:

1. You set up a management plan for your financial portfolio.

    - By doing this you can focus on being truly wealthy or thinking of other people rather than just being wealthy and thinking of yourself and what you want.

2. You set up a protection plan for your financial portfolio.

    - By doing this you can focus on being truly wealthy or thinking of other people rather than just being wealthy and thinking of yourself and what you want.

3. You follow the fundamental principles of being truly rich.

    - By doing this you can focus on being truly wealthy or thinking of other people rather than just being wealthy and thinking of yourself and what you want.

4. You share with other people what you know about how you succeeded in becoming truly wealthy.

5. You teach other people what you know. You refer people to The Legacy Journal Collection <> How To Become Truly Successful and other good books:

$$$
The Power Of Having Financial Freedom
$$$

Volume One
How To Become TRULY Rich
Released in 2008 to the general public

Volume Two
How To Become TRULY Wealthy
Released in 2009 to the general public

Volume Three
How To Become TRULY Rich As A Kid
or more commonly referred to as:
How To Help Your Kids Become TRULY Rich
Released in 2016 to the general public

6. You don't keep your ideas of success a secret.

    - You are always looking for ways to help other people.

7. You willingly give of your time, talents and financial means in helping other people to be successful too.

8. You help the poor out. In this case helping those who truly want to be helped.

    - You can try to help those that don't want your help, but this is rarely successful in the long term.

    - You help those that are truly poor. The truly poor meaning those that are stuck and would appreciate your help, not your handout.

9. To be truly wealthy you need to actually set-up your own charity foundations or humanitarian organizations and truly make a difference with your life, Your family's life and the lives of countless others.

    - You need to start looking for opportunities to become truly wealthy by creating actual volunteer programs.

    - You are a volunteer too, but what you are really looking for are volunteers to work with you.

        o You create opportunities for other people to volunteer through your volunteer programs.

            - Here are some examples of volunteer programs that already exist:

                ✓ Red Cross
                ✓ United Way
                ✓ Hospitals
                ✓ Schools
                ✓ Church Humanitarian Services
                ✓ Community Care and Share
                ✓ Community Firemen
                ✓ Neighborhood Watch
                ✓ Community Big Brother
                ✓ Community Big Sister
                ✓ Other Charity or Humanitarian Organizations
                ✓ Etc...

10. You may be interested in making a difference in some political arena.

    - Politics is another source of volunteering. In this case, you aren't creating opportunities for other people to volunteer. You are volunteering yourself.

        o Don't get involved in politics if you are doing it for your own personal gain, because you will only end up hurting a lot of people, as you selfishly make decisions that benefit you.

        o Get involved in politics if you are willing to help other people by being the voice of the people.

    - You are volunteering to help other people by representing them in helping them improve, succeed and be protected.

        o Here are some examples of various politically opportunities:

            ✓ School Board
            ✓ City Mayor
            ✓ City Council
            ✓ County Commissioner
            ✓ State Governor
            ✓ State Legislator
            ✓ President of your country
            ✓ Federal Legislator
            ✓ House of Representative
            ✓ Prime Minister
            ✓ Parliament
            ✓ Ambassador representing your country
            ✓ Federal Cabinet appointment
            ✓ State Supreme Court
            ✓ Federal Supreme Court
            ✓ Etc…

11. You can set up synergizing organizations, groups, clubs or councils. You can call them what you may.

    - The objective is to create an atmosphere where people can get together to synergize in positive ways and in doing positive things.

    - You will want your group to have an atmosphere of educating each other.

    - In your group, you want people that are influential thinkers, paradigm thinkers and problem solvers.

- In your group, you don't want people that are stuck on only using old solutions or strategies.

What you pursue as a group depends on you and possibly where you live. The sky is the limit for the good that your group can do.

Remember, you can't solve all of the world's problems, but you sure can make a difference.

Being truly wealthy is making a difference in the lives of other people around you.

Being truly wealthy means that you have the time and the means to make a difference in the world and you are doing it.

$$$$$

**THIS SPACE IS FOR YOUR
FURTHER JOURNAL NOTES ON CHAPTER 2:**

Chapter 3

WHAT HAS WEALTH DONE TO THE HUMAN RACE?

WEALTH IN HISTORY

HISTORY IS A GOOD TEACHER!!!

$$$$$$$$$

- What does history have to do with being wealthy?

    o History can tell the difference between truly succeeding and failing at being wealthy.

- What can and do history books have to say about the past, present and the future when it comes to wealth and wealth building?

    o History helps us to learn from the past, in order to understand the present and in turn to determine the future.

- Where do you fit in with history?

    o You need to be the judge of that question.

1. In history who were the rich and wealthy in the world and in particular in Europe?

- In ancient times the rich and wealthy were landlords, which include the royal families, kingdoms, principalities, empires, dynasties and tribes. These have come and gone over the time of written history as major powers of control and governmental systems. In most cases an individual or family ruled the people of their various time periods.

- In more recent times, in order to get away from individual or family rule, the power has shifted to major groups. This is a way to involve anyone that wants to join in, instead of a select few running things. It's become a more people-oriented society of systems. It at least gives the people some kind of hope.

2. Is hope just another deception in appearing to appease the majority of people into thinking that they too are a part of the game of politics, government rule and control?

- Recent history appears to be a little bit of both, genuine sincerity and deception.
    - You need to be the judge, because you are going to have to decide where you want to fit into today's governing economic systems.

3. How and why did the wealthy depend on slavery so prominently in history?

- In the history books a major sign of wealth also included human slavery or owning people as a part of a landlord's possessions.

- The Egyptians, the Romans, the tribes of the Native Americans and Native Africans all practiced this form of control or indebtedness traditionally referred to as slavery. The sad note is that they did it to each other or to their own race, relative or neighbor.

- European civilized societies practiced slavery, but they called their slaves, peasants and sometimes servants. The landowner owned more than just land and things; he also owned the people on his land. From the indentured servants to the fiefs who worked the fields couldn't go anywhere or do anything without the written permission of their landlord. Death was not an uncommon result if caught without permission and of course the consequence was determined by the landlord.

    o There were two types of peasants, the fief and the freeman. Both worked the land, but the freeman wasn't owned by the landlord. They were free to work for any landowner, just as long as they had written permission from their previous landlord to leave and work elsewhere. In other words, a landowner had to first claim them. The freeman was only free to move about, with permission of course, but the fiefs always stayed where they were. A fief's only hope was to someday prove themselves worthy by their landlord to grant them freeman status.

4. What caused a major shift in wealth, power and control to take place after the Crusades of Europe?

- From the Crusades of Europe there became established trade routes ultimately giving rise to a new group of people known as tradesmen. The tradesmen became what are now called merchants. These early merchants accidentally found a foothold over the landlords throughout Europe. Greedy landlords wanted more of the unique and fine quality things from Asia Minor and the merchants were more than happy to get it for them.

- Like an addition, the need for more became the norm throughout Europe. The landlords forgot to keep watch over their kingdoms and in time they became indebted to the merchants.

    o This thing called greed has been with us ever since. The addition of wanting more and more and more and more, etc. Even to the point of intoxication. It became a way of life.

5. What happened to the wealthy after the Crusades?

- After the Crusades a new class of people began to emerge, the traders of exotic goods or later known as merchants. These people didn't own land, but had something that the landowners wanted and would pay dearly for. The freemen began migrating from the fields to the towns and villages where they could work for the merchants.

- After hundreds of years these merchants actually became wealthier financially than their counter parts, the landlords. In time these merchants wanted a say in matters too. To appease the merchants the landlords began giving them rights of governing power in the various towns and villages, thus the new forms of government, similar to today's systems, took hold.

6. There became two forms of rich groups or classes of rich, the merchants and the landlords. All was good and well, but in time the merchants wanted more. They wanted land too. The problem was that there was no land for sale and no landlord was about to give up their land. If the landlord did sell their land, they'd lose all of their riches, in other words their power and control, thus their freedom and independence.

   - The Age of Discovery sets in with the merchants leading out. Around the world they go. It's easier to take from someone you don't know and will never see again.

     o During the Age of Discovery, the power of the various European countries began their empire building.

     o During this time the freemen were becoming no longer in debt. They were starting to buy their own little shops. They too, wanted a say in matters. What they got was the freedom of **the fiefs** from the landlords in order to provide workers in the cities to help the merchants.

     o In Europe slavery is now gone.

     o The fiefs were now the only peasants or people in debt to someone else. They had no say. They just worked where they could for survival. They were a dime a dozen, thus meager wages. At least they could move about, if they could find a job, that is.

7. How did the wealthy try to control the people?

- Now there seems to be three classes of people throughout Europe. The wealthy, landowners and merchants, then the small shop owners, and finally the employed peasants or new form of slavery. In today's terms, it's the upper class, middle class and lower class or in other words, the wealthy, rich and poor or those that are independent, free and in debt.

    o There really is another class, as there was back then and always has been the unemployed or the potentially extremely poor or totally dependent on others for their survival.

- In more recent times the Industrial Revolution took over the place of farming and the mega power of the landlords was gone. Mass production sets in. Make more and more products and thus the price goes down and then more people are able to afford to buy the products.

    o Factories and assembly lines became the task master to the peasants. Now the peasant gets the new title of employee. Wow, prestige. What more could a fellow ask for?

    o Employees did grow to large numbers and thus the concept of unions took hold. Unions represent the large scale of employees. Typically benefits were what the unions were after, such as equal rights, fair trade, labor laws and employee housing. Now the unions are more about higher wages.

- The problems of today still haven't changed, just the titles and of course a few more benefits.

    o In the past, all of this was great, but the employee was still dependent on the employer.

    o In the past, the merchants got a new title, now referred to as employer.

    o What's the problem? Employees are still in debt to someone else for their survival. They must have an employer in order to keep them alive.

8. Why does history appear to be a little bit of both, genuine sincerity and deception?

    - Once again recent history appears to be a little bit of both genuine sincerity and deception.

        o You need to be the judge, because you are going to have to decide where you want to fit into today's governing economic systems.

9. Why were large groups allowed to try and step into the shoes of the wealthy?

- The rise in recent times of group run governments or political societies evolved in order to thwart off individuals from having too much power and control due to their wealth.

- For example, capitalism was based on the creation of new things. The newer things people come up with or create the more people end up getting rich. Anyone can do it was the idea behind capitalism. Capitalism was meant to involve anyone and everyone within their many and varied ways and means of doing things.

    o The newer things that are created also provide jobs for the masses of people that haven't figured out that they too could be creative and get rich too.

    o It sounds like an ideal situation for anyone and everyone. Everybody seems to benefit in some way within capitalism. It's basically up to you in how much you want to do.

    o Capitalism couldn't work in the distant past due to the various types of governments that existed back then that wouldn't allow the people to have a say about anything. That's why capitalism is a fairly new way of doing things and is evolving even now.

- Communism is also a new concept. It's most noted with the fall of the Old Russian Empire that was ruled for hundreds of years by a few families. The question for Old Russia was what political system should take the place of the rule of the czar and his family?

- o Freedom for all of the people was the war cry. Just like the American's war cry.

- o Many ideas were thrown about, but no one idea really stepped up to the plate to take charge until an activist named Lenin. He really started out with more of a socialistic approach. As time went by there was still great chaos among the people, thus something had to be done to put some kind of order or control over the rebellious masses. What began to appear was a new form of government known as communism.

- o Communism is based on the principle of everyone being treated equal. It sounds good. It at least brought the people together. It gave the people an illusion of hope.

- o As country they now had a purpose. Everybody pitched in to make it work. No one was to be left behind. There will be no rich or poor. The leaders of the new nation will lead the way. Follow your leaders.

- o After some time passed Lenin passed away. A new leader takes over by the name of Stalin. He adds one more element to solidify communism. If the people didn't do what he wanted done they'd be killed. Million were killed. Thus no one dared to break rank.

- o Yes, the people were still considered equal to each other, but most of the profit from the people who labored went to the governing few. The government made sure everybody had a job. That's what communism was about, right?

- o The people were not considered citizens, so they had no voting right or say in anything. Citizens were the governing few. You were invited to become a citizen if you proved yourself well. The governing body of communism became a new class of people. Basically, you were in the military or associated with it in some way or you were a commoner. Either you were a pretend rich person or a poor person or in other words a common person with no rights or privileges.

I personally don't see any difference between communism and the past forms of governments and economic outlooks. About the only difference, I really see, was that communism was run by a group of individuals, kind of like a senate or a congress. From that group one would be chosen to lead or represent the group.

- Another new idea came along called socialism, which is much like communism. The purpose was for all people to be treated equally and for all people to have a job provided by the government.

- **The difference between socialism and communism was that in socialism the government wouldn't own everything. The people could own their homes, go where they wanted to and the people could decide what they wanted to make in their neighborhood, government owned factories. Part of the profits would be shared equally with the factory employees and the rest of the profits went to the government.**

- In communism, there wasn't much of an incentive to work hard or to try and get ahead. It just wasn't going to happen. In socialism, it was worth it to work hard as a factory or group because you, as a group, could get ahead. Your ideas for improving things were welcomed too.

- There are still many countries in the world today that use the socialistic economic system.

- In both communism and socialism, the government is to provide some form of basic medical care. Socialism seemed to do better in the area of medical care, partly because the people had some say in it.

- Major military force to get things done, according to socialistic government wishes, has been kept to a minimum in most socialistic societies, at least to this point in time in history.

- The concern with socialism is that the government could turn against its people for any reason and at any time, because the few in government still have the ultimate control and say over the people.

- Socialism appears to be better than most of the older forms of government where only a few people ruled the masses of people.

10. What's the difference between capitalism, communism and socialism?

- In communism, you progress as a whole or you don't progress at all. In socialism, you progress as a group and the group can only go as far as the government allows the group to go. In capitalism, you progress as an individual and can go as far as you want, capable of and able to.

- Capitalism is the only one of the three major governments and economic systems that allows the people to decide what they do, how much they do and to be governed by either the rich or the poor.

- In capitalism, the trick in getting elected as an official has to do with the ability in proving yourself to the people and if the people are satisfied with your performance, you get to continue running the affairs of the various levels of government. If the people aren't satisfied with your performance, then you are voted out or in other words, gone.

- Capitalism also differs from communism and socialism where it affects the people that live within its society. In a capitalistic society, the individual is ultimately responsible for him or herself, not the government.

- In capitalism, the individual takes care of his or her own medical needs, not the government. Unions have helped individuals in negotiating medical insurance coverage for their employees as a benefit, typically instead of paying the employee more.

- In capitalism, the government doesn't take care of the people.

- The government is supposed to regulate safety and fairness and to keep the peace. It can act as a temporary support group, but the key is temporary.

- Minimum intrusion is the philosophy behind capitalism.

11. What has happened to America?

- You will notice that America today doesn't seem to fit any of the three economic and governmental systems as just described. It seems to be more of a mix in the America of today.

    o Where's America headed?

    o What do the history books have to say about where America's been and how it's gotten to where it is today?

- o In other words, where are you headed?

- America used to declare itself as a capitalistic governing society and boasted of that fact.

- America sounds more and more like a socialistic society than a capitalistic society.

  - o One big shift in American history took place when the government introduced the national welfare program. It was supposed to be a temporary help. It never was supposed to become a part of the American fabric. The depression really took its toll and the people needed help until things got better. The welfare system never left America, so that is a sign that America's been living in some form of a socialistic state for many decades.

  - o Now people in America are crying for medical care for every citizen in this country. That simply means more socialistic control or socialism.

  - o True, people need help, but think about what the people are giving up.

  - o America was based on independence and freedom to do what you want and being able to take care of yourself, without someone else telling you what you can and can't do.

  - o In a capitalistic society, you have to step up and take care of yourself. Life isn't free, but the freedom to do and choose what you want is still in your hand and is up to you.

  - o In a capitalistic society, the more you do the easier it becomes. The more benefits you can get, because you provide the benefits for yourself.

12. Have the people of America become so poor that they can't take care of themselves anymore?

- You need to be the judge, because you are going to have to decide where you want to fit into today's governing economic systems, which will also be the determining factor of what type of systems will be available in the future.

13. What system seems to work for you, if you want to be truly rich or truly wealthy?

        Communism   Or   Socialism   Or   Capitalism   Why?

- Each political and economic system has its pros and cons.

    o It basically comes down to whether you want to take care of yourself or not.

- In the future I think working together is very important too. You really can't go it alone or do it on your own.

- I'm concerned for the future when it comes to survival. It looks more and more like a dog-eat-dog world out there.

    o To me the future appears to be the survival of the fittest. I'm not talking about physical strength. I'm talking about financial strength or in other words the ability to take care of yourself.

14. Let's look back at Communism, Socialism and Capitalism. I think all three systems have some good merits that should be considered in the future. Learning from and finding what worked and what didn't work is a good place to start when considering the future.

    - Communism's basic philosophy is that every person is to be treated equally. No rich or poor. In other words, everybody is treated fairly or the same.

    - Socialism's basic philosophy is teamwork. In other words, everybody working together and benefiting together.

    - Capitalism's basic philosophy is that every person is independent and can go as far in life as he or she puts the effort into his or her life. In other words, everybody is free to accomplish what they want.

    - Three positive ideas put together are much better than one or another trying to survive on its own in the future.

15. Can all three basic philosophies work together to make a better future?
Yes Or No Why?

- You will have to be the final judge on this question. As for me, I believe all three have good merits and qualities or characteristics that can work together and benefit each other if done in selfless ways. Selfishness has been the downfall of each of these systems in the past.

    o **Equality:**
    - You can feel like you are all on the same playing field.

    o **Independence:**
    - You can decide what you are going to do, accomplish and then motivate yourself to do it.

    o **Teamwork:**
    - You can accomplish more when working together.

16. What other ideas can you come up with that would be worthy to take forward into the future?

- Hopefully you have a better understanding of how we got to where we are today.

17. Where does a wealthy person fit in the future of mankind and their future history?

- It's truly up to a wealthy person, if he or she is willing to be unselfish.

18. Where do you fit in the future of mankind and their future history?

- It's truly up to you, if you are unselfish about it.

Refer to the companion book "How to Become Truly Rich" from The Legacy Journal Collection <> How To Become Truly Successful for further discussion on this matter.

Remember, you can't solve all of the world's problems, but you sure can make a difference.

Being truly wealthy is making a difference in the lives of other people around you.

Being truly wealthy means that you have the time and the means to make a difference in the world and you are doing it.

$$$$$$$$$

**THIS SPACE IS FOR YOUR
FURTHER JOURNAL NOTES ON CHAPTER 3:**

Chapter 4

HOW CAN A TRULY WEALTHY PERSON BE A LEADER?

<u>BE AN EXAMPLE</u>

WHAT DO YOU HAVE TO OFFER OTHER PEOPLE?

$$$$$$$$$

- Do you have what it takes to make a difference?   Yes   or   No   Why?

- How can you make a difference?

If you are truly wealthy all eyes are going to be on you. That is just a part of the territory that comes with being truly wealthy. You can try and hide from it or you can do something good with it. You can make a difference.

In your situation, you can do more good with less effort than anyone else can. That's just the way it is. That's why if you are wealthy, you are really needed. Other people are important to, but sometimes it's the one that happens to be in the right spot at the right time that can do the most good that gets the call that can make a difference.

There is some strange thing about peers or equals not giving each other due respect or attention as they would to someone that is over them. If you've got the money, you've got the attention of other people as if you are over them. Other people will tend to do more for you than they would for their own peers.

Keep in mind that you can be in a position to make a difference in how people learn to treat each other in regard to respect and attention they give to each other. By modeling to other people, through your example and teaching or showing respect for other people, you too can lead the way to a better society.

> **Make a difference!**

> **Change behaviors!**

- Teach other people that it's all in how you look at things!

    o Get people to understand that it's okay to quit complaining, ridiculing, back biting, threatening, blaming and just coping along the way.

    o Get people to understand that it's okay to be accepting, helping out, seeing things from another perspective and trying it out, telling someone thanks, saying you are sorry or asking someone for forgiveness.

- **How do you teach someone how to behave?**

1st You start with your own example. You model appropriate behavior.

2nd You complement any good behavior that you see other people doing.

3rd You tell other people how much you appreciate certain types of good, appropriate, acceptable or professional behaviors.

4th You tell other people why certain behaviors are best and what kinds of impact you see from such behaviors and what good they are producing.

Don't reward people for good behavior. If you reward people for good behavior, it won't become a sustainable or permanent behavior. People will change when they see other types of results, because of their improved behavior. How they are treated is how they will want to treat you.

Send cues or signals that will trigger certain behaviors, reactions or actions. When other people knowingly or unknowingly get these cues or signals repeated to them at certain times they will respond the same way each time. Keep sending out the cues or signals by your examples until you see the other people responding the way you would like them to behave. Practice makes perfect, so the more good behavior cues you give the sooner you will see people change until it becomes a habit for them to respond this way or that way depending on the cues or signals that are around them.

Create a positive atmosphere for yourself and those that are around you. You will like it and they will too.

- How do you teach someone how to accept, change or to improve?

1st The key is to get the other person to buy in on the idea.

- People have to take ownership in the idea.
- People need to want to see things through a different set of eyes.

2nd Find out what the other person is interested in.

- People have to have a reason to want to join in.
- Selfish people won't change until they see a need or a reason to change.

3rd Create a starting point or comfort zone for the other person.

- Help those that truly want your help and then you will affect change.
- You can't help those that don't want to change, but you do it anyway realizing the expectations may not be the same.
- Progress is totally dependent on the willingness of the other person.

4th Create the big picture for the other person.

- Objective   –   Purpose
- Results   –   Expectations
- Outcome   –   Benefits

5th Have the other person demonstrate from their own understanding or perspective what he or she sees and their desired outcome.

- The more you can involve the other person the sooner he or she will catch on and take ownership or master whatever it is you are trying to teach or accomplish.

- **What do you teach other people?**

1st You want other people to know fundamental and true principles to live by and to be governed by.

- You teach the truth.
- You live by the truth.
- You stand by the truth.

2nd Here are some of the most important elements you need to understand in order to make sure you understand yourself and why you do what you do and how to always do things better or best in the future.

3rd The following are fundamental principles that must be properly understood and, in turn, lived by in order to be truly wealthy:

A. **Believe**

- Believing is to accept a fact or something that you know to be true, but not necessarily act on it.

B. **Faith**

- Faith is the act of doing something that you believe in.
- Faith means more than acceptance, it means action.
- Action means work and work means productivity and productivity means results.

C. **Hope**

- Hope is the assurance of knowing what a person believes in or has accepted and has faith in or acted on is true and never changing.
- To be assured is the ability to endure.

- Hope is the ability to endure with purpose or for an end result.

D. Trust

- Trust is the key ingredient that motivates a person to move forward or act on something.

E. Commitment

- Commitment is the same thing as obedience, such as to be obedient to the laws or principles that govern whatever you believe in, such as what you stand for.

- You do something, because you believe in it.

F. Sacrifice

- Sacrifice is to forgo getting something or giving away something of yours.

- You sacrifice for a purpose or a better end result.

G. Forgive

- Forgiving is to let go of wrongs that were done to you or to not be consumed by the wrongs and move on with your life.

H. Apologize

- Apologizing is to seek forgiveness or to correct a wrong where possible.

I. Truth

- Truth is based on facts or in other words on what cannot change. It's dependable, long lasting or forever.

J. Understanding

- Understanding is the desire to know the truth. Not just the parts you might want to believe or accept, but the truth and nothing but the truth.

- Understanding is also symbolic of patience or caring, which results once a person has a full understanding of a situation or is governed by truth and facts and accepts them.

K. **Wisdom**
- Wisdom is the ability to seek the truth wherever it may be.

- Wisdom is the ability to live by the truth.

- Wisdom is the ability to see the difference between what is right and what is wrong.

- Wisdom is the ability to choose the right.

L. **Humility**

- Humility is the ability to be humble enough to accept and live by the truth.

➢ **These are powerful principles that in order to be truly wealthy you must learn to understand each of them and apply them in your personal life and in everything you do.**

➢ **These principles are the pillars of success.**

➢ **Living by these principles can be one of the reasons or factors between why some people are truly wealthy and some people are poor.**

- How do you lead other people?

1st You lead by following the lead of the other person you are trying to help.

- You accept wherever the person is at in their individual life and go from there.

- You are finding the cues or signals that work best for each individual according to how he or she responds and is accepting.

- You can't make someone do something he or she doesn't agree with, doesn't accept or doesn't want to do.

2nd You lead by example with a loving and caring heart for the another person.

- If you are trying to get someone to do something, because it's what you want to do, neither of you will go very far. The other person has to want to do it too. If you care about someone enough you will have a heart of patience and understanding and realize that it's not all about you all of the time.

- If you care about someone you will wait for him or her to come around to realizing the benefits of what it is you want to do and then both of you will move forward together in positive ways.

- If you care enough about someone and you see that he or she doesn't understand the benefits, doesn't agree with you or doesn't want to do what you want to do that you are willing to accept him or her in whatever he or she is willing to accept and do and have fun while doing that much together.

3rd You lead by teaching amiable techniques to the other person.

- You teach the importance of consensus, unity, coming together and finding common ground in whatever you do.

- You teach the importance of doing things with love and care in whatever you do.

- You teach the importance of making decisions with loving intent and care in whatever you do.

- You teach the importance of making lasting progress, be it large or small, is more beneficial than power surges in progress that comes and goes in what you do.

- You teach the importance of stability, consistency, dependability and trust in what you do.

- You teach the importance of using any and all kinds of resources, which is a good thing to do in what you do.

- You teach the importance of seeking help in finding those that know how to make a change actually happen in what you do.

- You teach the importance of getting the big picture of whatever you are doing and then reducing and simplifying it down to something that is palatable, simple and manageable, which is a good thing to do in what you do.

- You teach the importance of creating, finding and using competent skills that can be used with multiple challenges and purposes in what you do.

- You teach the importance of how to persuade in positive ways, not in negative ways, such as coaxing, guilt trips, force or demanding in what you do.

- You teach the importance of how to persuade in positive ways by using the right kinds of words in what you say and do.

- You teach the importance of how to persuade in positive ways by figuring out and finding who the person you are trying to persuade is willing to accept, listen to or follow and that is the person in whom you work through in accomplishing the most good in what you do.

- You teach the importance of doing all that you can do, but realizing that as you are doing all that you can that it's okay and good to not try to do it all by yourself, but by realizing you can accomplish much more by working together with other resourceful people as a team in what you do.

All of these leadership attributes, skills and techniques should be applied within yourself first, to your family next, then with your business associates, both in non-profit and profit-making relationships and finally to anyone that may work under you, for you or along-side you.

I am sure you already have many great skills and attributes that you have used to get to this point in your successful life and I recommend you write them down if you haven't already. Compare your list with the examples I've just gone over and see which match up and what you seriously need to consider adding to your list.

- Go down your new list and write down your feelings as you ask yourself why you believe that technique is important to you.

    o After you have written your feelings about each one on your list, then go back and think of examples of when you used each technique and write those examples down.

    o Keep your list and add to it as you discover more tangible attributes, skills and techniques that are based on true principles and bring about goodwill.

Refer to the companion book "How to Become Truly Rich" from The Legacy Journal Collection<> How To Become Truly Successful for further discussion on this matter.

Remember, you can't solve all of the world's problems, but you sure can make a difference.

Being truly wealthy is making a difference in the lives of other people around you.

Being truly wealthy means that you have the time and the means to make a difference in the world and you are doing it.

$$$$$$$$$

**THIS SPACE IS FOR YOUR
FURTHER JOURNAL NOTES ON CHAPTER 4:**

Chapter 5

HOW DOES A TRULY WEALTHY PERSON CREATE SUSTAINABLE SYNERGY?

THINK TANKS

CAN YOU TAKE WHAT'S IN YOUR MIND AND TURN IT INTO REALITY?

$$$$$$$$$

> ➤ **Synergizing is what makes the world go around!**

You need to set up a synergy organization, group, club or council. Call it what you may. As a truly wealthy person you want to help other people out and what better way than to get people involved along with you in some kind of worthwhile organization.

- What does synergize mean or what is its objective?

People that get together to synergize come together to solve problems, come up with solutions or create new ideas and how to implement them. That is what synergizing is all about. Synergizing is nothing more than a think tank or group of people coming together and working together.

True, some things your **synergy** group will come up with will potentially generate untold amounts of money and other things may have nothing to do with making money. Your group may have many things going on at the same time. That's a good thing to get to synergize about as a synergy group.

Whatever you do let the positive synergy lead you to what's important at the time, be it money making or helping mankind out. A synergy group can accomplish many good and great things in the world and in whatever arena the group wants to focus on.

Don't forget that the more people are involved in a synergizing group the potential for more good that can be done by that group.

- One head is good, but how much better are many heads working together?

With a synergizing group the objective is to create an atmosphere where people can get together to synergize in positive ways. Separate contention from the group. It doesn't lead anywhere. If you find discord in your group, make an exit plan to weed it out of the group. Politics seems to be the place for such people to go who want to be a part of negative bantering.

Synergizing as a group is a form of educating each other. You want your group to have an atmosphere of educating each other. For someone to give a presentation to other people that are interested in learning and applying what they learned is a real mind builder for all involved. You want to see other people anxious to learn about something and then report back to the group what they found out.

In your group, you will want people that are influential thinkers, paradigm thinkers and problem solvers. In your group, you don't want people that are stuck on only using old solution methods or strategies they knew and used in the past. Have an exit plan for those that can't go beyond what's in front of them. They aren't really interested in making a difference. They like where they are stuck at and really only want to stay there. You also don't want criticizers or people that spend their time putting down other people and/or other ideas.

What you pursue as a group depends on you and possibly where you live. The sky is the limit for the good that your group can do.

- Why haven't I suggested for you to just join another group that is already in existence?

If you are truly wealthy you have the time, talents and means to do more than just follow someone else's lead. If you are truly wealthy you can join another group that is already in place, but if you are wealthy, you are in a position to make an even more powerful difference in the world. You can do more than just belong to a club that gets together once in a while and may accomplish something or maybe not. You can do more by creating your own group and hand picking the people involved in the group. Make sure you have a group of people that can bring to the table different talents, contacts and ways of getting things done.

If you do decide to join a group that already exists, then make sure it meets the type of expectations that I have outlined. There is nothing wrong with getting involved with a high synergy group that is already truly making a major impact. The problem is that there probably aren't that many groups to be found in a typical community.

- **Make a difference!**

- **Have an influence for good!**

- **Be a leader!**

Remember, you can't solve all of the world's problems, but you sure can make a difference.

Being truly wealthy is making a difference in the lives of other people around you.

Being truly wealthy means that you have the time and the means to make a difference in the world and you are doing it.

$$$$$$$$$

**THIS SPACE IS FOR YOUR
FURTHER JOURNAL NOTES ON CHAPTER 5:**

Chapter 6

CHARITY, IS IT IN YOU?

HUMANITARIAN SERVICE

IF YOU WANT TO RECEIVE, THEN BE WILLING TO GIVE!!!

$$$$$$$$$

- The key to being truly wealthy is the willingness to give.

    o Some people just can't give. They can blame genetics, circumstances from where they live or the way they were raised, but it doesn't matter, because it's who they are now.

- We are a "**me first**" society.

    o There just isn't any room for anyone else in, "me."

- Charity of the heart is a foreign concept to most people. Why, because most people have grown up in a dog-eat-dog environment of survival.

    o Charity of the heart almost has to be retrained into someone, because he or she doesn't know any better.

It is understandable if you don't have something to give away to someone else if you don't have anything to give in the first place. However, there is one thing that can be given away, no matter who you are and that is yourself, your time and talents.

If you are wealthy, you not only have the time and talents to give, but you also have the means. How did a wealthy person get their means or wealth? More than likely off of the backs of people you used and now could use a little bit of your help in return. That in and of itself is a good reason to give back to those that made it possible for you to acquire your wealth.

If you truly want to rise up above the crowd of mayhem, loss and confusion it isn't by being wealthy, it's by helping others to rise up with you. If you want to rise up to the stars, then you need to help others to rise up above the crowd. As you help other people rise up to be successful, you too can rise up from wherever you are to greater levels of experience and self-worth.

You can't make yourself successful. It's other people that make you successful. You can try all you want and you may even find that you made it to the top, but your chance of staying there is small without the help of other people keeping you there. The more people that rise with you the more there will be around you in a binding and worthwhile way. It's a win-win relationship, friendship and support group of people helping people.

What has been missing in the history books of the wealthy are the truly sustainable characteristics of a truly wealthy person. These are the traits that endear people to each other and establish a lasting legacy. It's about the goodness of a person. It's about the genuine selflessness of an individual. History likes to glorify a person's heroic triumph or deed, but the person himself is lost in history. What he thinks, believes in or why he is motivated to do the deed is overlooked and more importantly greater deeds of everyday living are what bring a person to the point of notoriety are hardly ever brought out. Such traits and little things are what make the person who he is and is what is most needed in order to model for future posterities in how to be truly successful, however that is what is typically missing in history books.

Charity is the key ingredient or characteristic that must be developed within a wealthy person if he or she wants to create a lasting legacy of being truly wealthy that can withstand the test of time.

- **What is charity?**

    o Charity *is* **love**.

    o Charity is **action**.

    o Charity is the **desire to give**.

    o Charity is the desire to **give of one's self**.

- **What is love?**
    - Love is the **desire to care**.
    - Love is the **desire to share**.
    - Love is the **desire to comfort**.

A truly wealthy person has developed these traits of the characteristics of charity, which inspires a truly wealthy person in what to do with their wealth, time, talents and means.

Charity is what gives a truly wealthy person purpose, which is based on the 12 fundamental principles of:

1. **Believe**
2. **Faith**
3. **Hope**
4. **Trust**
5. **Commitment**
6. **Sacrifice**
7. **Forgive**
8. **Apologize**
9. **Truth**
10. **Understanding**
11. **Wisdom**
12. **Humility**

- **What does it mean to be a humanitarian?**

    o Humanitarian is the idea of a human or a person giving service to someone or something else in order to help out, to improve upon, to cause to rise up to change or to make a difference.

    o Humanitarian service is the idea of a person doing something out of charity.

- **What does it mean to give service?**

  o Service is the act of and willingness to do something for and in behalf of someone or something else.

  o Service is the idea of giving of time, talents and means to someone or something else that may be less fortunate or in need.

- **What does it mean to volunteer?**

    o Volunteering is the act and willingness to do something for and in behalf of someone or something else as a service.

    o Volunteering is the idea of giving of time, talents and means to someone or something else that may be less fortunate or in need as a service.

    o Volunteering is the act of taking someone or something else's place in doing something for and on behalf of someone or something else.

- **What does it mean to, "have heart" or "from the heart?"**

  o When the word heart is used by a person it is referring to a person's feelings, emotions, personal desires or inner desires, etc.

The following are a list of some examples of feelings of the heart you can have:

- **Do you have <u>love</u> in your heart?**

- **Do you have a <u>caring</u> heart?**

- **Do you have <u>charity</u> in your heart?**

- **Do you have <u>humanitarian</u> feelings in your heart?**

- **Do you have feelings of <u>service</u> in your heart?**

- **Do you have <u>volunteering</u> feelings in your heart?**

These are the feelings that make the difference between a wealthy person and a truly wealthy person.

- **Which feelings do you have?**

- **Which feelings do you want to have? Why?**

- **Which feelings are you going to have?**

- **Which feelings do you need to work on or improve on in order for you to be truly wealthy? Why?**

Remember, you can't solve all of the world's problems, but you sure can make a difference.

Being truly wealthy is making a difference in the lives of other people around you.

Being truly wealthy means that you have the time and the means to make a difference in the world and you are doing it.

$$$$$$$$$

**THIS SPACE IS FOR YOUR
FURTHER JOURNAL NOTES ON CHAPTER 6:**

Chapter 7

WHAT ELSE DO YOU CARE ABOUT?

CHARITY OF ANOTHER KIND

CHARITY IS THE TRUE SIGN OF HUMANITY!!!

$$$$$$$$$

> ➢ In the following space make a list of the things that are important to you. You can put anything on your list. It doesn't matter so much at this point in what is on your list as it does that you create some kind of a list of things that are important to you.

➢ From your list of things that are important to you, can you see any that may be important to other people?

Yes   or   No

- In the following space list those items that you see may be important to other people too.

- In the following space make a list of who some of these, "other people" are.

➢ Do you consider some of these, "other people" as wealthy individuals?

Yes   or   No

If you've been able to make a list of some, "other people" then you are on the right track. You can consider either getting involved with such individuals and some of the things that are important to them, by joining their group/s or creating your own group and inviting such individuals to be involved with you in doing something that is important to you as well as what could well be important to them too.

> Do you consider some of these, "other people" as poor or in need of a helping hand? Yes or No

    o If you do consider some of these people as poor, **but are trying to make a difference in their circumstance or some situation or cause,** then you are on the right track.

    o Sometimes such individuals have an insight to what actually needs to be done or that can be done and/or are already involved where they can and in doing what they can.

One way or another, you will have some possible projects that you could get involved in by joining in with other people in their individual needs and/or projects or joining in with existing humanitarian organizations and/or you may have some of your own possible projects to consider develop into doing as humanitarian projects of your own.

If you aren't satisfied with what you came up with on your own, then the following is a list of some other possible general humanitarian areas that you could consider in getting involved in by either creating it yourself or joining in with other existing humanitarian organizations or groups that want to make a positive difference in the world in some way. It can be something that directly affects people or indirectly by affecting the earth and all that lives on it. One way or another it will sooner or later affect the people of this planet we live on:

1. Protect or improve the quality of the earth in order to preserve it.

2. Protect or improve the quality of the air in order to preserve it.

3. Protect or improve the quality of the water in order to preserve it.

4. Protect or improve the quality of life for the animals, birds and fish in order to preserve them.

5. Protect or improve the quality of the human race in order to preserve it.

One way or another you need to find an area or something that excites you in wanting to be involved in making a difference for the good of whatever your cause may be. If it is something that you are excited about, then it will take off, grow and/or develop into something worthwhile and helpful to others around you.

If you aren't satisfied with what you came up with on your own, then the following is a list of some other possible general humanitarian areas that you could consider that are examples of ways in which you could be involved, by either creating it yourself or joining in with other existing humanitarian organizations and providing such management or assistance that can make or break any organization opportunities for success. I would guess that the question would be, what can you bring to the table or what are your talents that would be of value and of benefit by you getting involved with an organization in promoting and doing some kind of good in the world where you live.

> Would you consider the following ideas as things that you could contribute in the way of some of your possible talents or expertise that could benefit a humanitarian organization? Yes or No Indicate which ones?

1. **Understanding**

    ✓ Help other people understand what the organization is all about.

    ✓ Organizations need some form of order in what they are trying to accomplish.

    ✓ Visual or Written examples and directions are a valuable tool to any organization.

2. **Interactive**

    ✓ Help other people by interacting with them so that they understand what the organization is all about.

    ✓ Organizations need someone to represent them by going out to the public and being the voice of the organization. You could be the Public Relations Person.

    ✓ Involve other people by being interactive with them. Show other people how they too can do it, just like you are doing it.

3. **Survival**

    ✓ Humanitarian organizations, just like any business, need help being able to survive the ups and downs that go along with any venture.

    ✓ Sometimes it is financial support and other times it is legal issues or a whole myriad of different things that can take down a venture.

4. **Quality**

    ✓ Humanitarian services, just like any business venture, needs quality people, products and service.

➢ If you have the know-how, then you are needed.

➢ If you have high integrity, high standards and high principles that govern your life, then you are needed.

These are just a few areas you should consider when looking for any organization to create or join in with. The integrity of which any organization is run is vital to its consumers and or benefactors.

If you are still looking for something to do, then try looking on the internet and see what you can find that is already out there in the way of things to do or organizations that you might want to consider in joining. Check with your community and see what is already going on in your neighborhood that you might consider getting involved with. You can also check with your community to see what some of their needs are and see if there might be something that you could actually take charge of and get started for your neighborhood.

Keep in mind that whatever you do now may change over time. The main thing is to get started in doing something and letting it evolve a little bit and see where it takes you. By getting your feet wet, in some way, you are well on your way to making a difference in whatever humanitarian service project you choose to pursue. You will be appreciated and looked up to by those in whom you give your trust to, because they too will give you their trust and all will grow together toward making this world a little better than it was the day before.

- What can you do to help any humanitarian organization survive and thrive?

- What are you going to do?

> Decide something and see where it leads you.

Remember, you can't solve all of the world's problems, but you sure can make a difference.

Being truly wealthy is making a difference in the lives of other people around you.

Being truly wealthy means that you have the time and the means to make a difference in the world and you are doing it.

$$$$$$$$$

**THIS SPACE IS FOR YOUR
FURTHER JOURNAL NOTES ON CHAPTER 7:**

Chapter 8

HOW DO YOU SET-UP YOUR OWN NON-PROFIT CHARITY ORGANIZATIONS?

CHARITY FROM THE HEART

WHY SHOULD YOU SET-UP YOUR OWN NON-PROFIT ORGANIZATIONS?

$$$$$$$$$

Charity organizations can be set up through different legal vehicles. The non-profit status is going to be under an umbrella in one of several ways.

1st   A foundation

2nd   A trust

3rd   An endowment

4th   An incorporation, which includes Inc., LC or LLC

A charity is a non-profit organization that is considered as a tax-exempt organization, which simply means the organization doesn't have to pay taxes on any money earned as an organization. The money stays with the organization to further its cause of goodwill and service for and on behalf of others and other things or places. If an individual were to receive an income from the organization as an employee of some sort, that individual would be liable to pay taxes on that particular income amount. The organization would not be liable to pay taxes on the amount that went to an employee.

To qualify for federal tax-exempt status under 501(c)(3) of the Internal Revenue Code, the non-profit organization must be organized and operate for some religious, educational, charitable, scientific, literary, testing for public safety, fostering of national or international amateur sports or prevention of cruelty to animals or children purpose permitted under this section of the code.

The following are some examples of advantages of a non-profit corporation:

- Directors are typically not personally responsible for the debts and liabilities of a nonprofit corporation.

- Nonprofit corporations have the ability to apply for both federal and state tax-exempt status.

- Certain nonprofit corporations are eligible to receive public and private grants, making the obtainment of operating capital easier.

- With 501(c)(3) nonprofits, donations made by individuals to the nonprofit corporation are tax-deductible to the individual.

In order to form a nonprofit corporation, you must create your non-profit articles of incorporation. In other words, a non-profit certificate of incorporation must be filed with the appropriate state agency and the necessary state filing fees paid.

The formation documents must include certain clauses and information, such as a very detailed business purpose statement, in order for the entity to qualify for tax-exempt status. Thereafter, form 1023 must be filed with the IRS.

The following is some tax-exempt status information to consider when setting up your organization:

From the IRS:

- Organizing Documents – Definition

    - Trust instrument, corporate charter, articles of incorporation, articles of association, or other written instrument by which the organization is created under state law.

- Disqualified Person – Definition

    - Provisions in legislation signed by the President on August 17, 2006, may affect the following information.

    - A disqualified person is any person who was in a position to exercise substantial influence over the affairs of the applicable tax-exempt organization at any time during the look back period. It is not necessary that the person actually exercise substantial influence, only that the person be in a position to do so.

    - Family members of the disqualified person and entities controlled by the disqualified person are also disqualified persons. For this purpose, the term control is defined as owning more than 35% of the voting power of a corporation, more than 35% of the profits interest in a partnership, or more than 35% of the beneficial interest in a trust.

- Charitable Solicitation – Explanation

    o Many states have laws regulating the <u>solicitation of funds</u> for charitable purposes. These statutes generally require organizations to <u>register</u> with a state agency before soliciting the state's residents for contributions, providing exemptions from registration for certain categories of organizations.

    o In addition, organizations may be required to file periodic financial reports. State laws may impose additional requirements on fundraising activity involving paid solicitors and fundraising counsel. An <u>IRS training document</u> describes these requirements in greater detail. Charitable organizations may wish to contact the appropriate state agency to learn more about the requirements that may apply in their state, before soliciting contributions. In some states, municipal or other local governments may also require organizations soliciting charitable contributions to register and report.

    o In addition to registration and reporting requirements associated with the solicitation of charitable contributions, some states require organizations to register and file periodic financial results if they hold assets subject to a charitable trust.

    o State Regulation of Charitable Solicitation and Registration Requirements to Hold Charitable Assets

        ▪ To determine in what state(s) you may be required to register to solicit charitable contributions or hold assets subject to a charitable trust, see the <u>website</u> of the National Association of State Charity Officials.

- Charitable Solicitation – Periodic Reporting

    o Most states have statutes that require charitable organizations that solicit contributions from the public to register and file periodic financial reports. See <u>State Charitable Solicitation Statutes</u> for a general discussion of these statutes. Many states accept a copy of the IRS <u>Form 990</u> in place of all or part of their financial report forms. If you use Form 990, Form 990-EZ, or 990-PF to satisfy state or local filing requirements, note the following -

Determine State Filing Requirements

You should consult the appropriate officials of all states and other jurisdictions in which the organization does business to determine their specific filing requirements. "Doing business" in a jurisdiction may include any of the following: (1) soliciting contributions or grants by mail or otherwise from individuals, businesses, or other charitable organizations; (b) conducting programs; (c) having employees within that jurisdiction; (d) maintaining a checking account; or (e) owning or renting property there

Monetary Tests May Differ

Dollar limitations applicable to Form 990, 990-EZ, or 990-PF, when filed with the IRS may not apply when using the return, in place of state or local report forms. Examples of IRS dollar limitations that do not meet some state requirements are the $25,000 gross receipts minimum that creates an obligation to file Form 990 or 990-EZ with the IRS and the $50,000 minimum for listing professional fees in Part II of Schedule A (Form 990, 990-EZ, or 990-PF).

Additional Information May Be Required

State or local filing requirements may require you to attach to Form 990, 990-EZ, or 990-PF, one or more of the following: (a) additional financial statements, such as a complete analysis of functional expenses or a statement of changes in net assets; (b) notes to financial statements; (c) additional financial schedules; (d) a report on the financial statements by an independent accountant; and (e) answers to additional questions and other information. Each jurisdiction may require the additional material to be presented on forms they provide. The additional information does not have to be submitted with the return filed with the IRS.

Even if IRS accepts the return that the organization files as complete, a copy of the same return filed with a state will not fully satisfy that state's filing requirement if required information is not provided, including any of the additional information discussed above, or if the state determines that the form was not completed by following the applicable Form 990, 990-EZ, or 990-PF instructions or supplemental state instructions, if so, the organization may be asked to provide the missing information or to submit an amended return.

Use of Audit Guides May Be Required

To ensure that all organizations report similar transactions uniformly, many states require that contributions, gifts, grants, etc., and functional expenses be reported according to the AICPA industry audit and accounting guide, *Not-for-Profit Organizations* (New York, NY, AICPA, 2003), supplemented by *Standards of Accounting and Financial Reporting for Voluntary Health and Welfare Organizations* (Washington, DC, National Health Council, Inc., 1998, 4th edition).

Donated Services And Facilities

Although the two publications named above sometimes call for reporting donated services and facilities as items of revenue and expenses, many states and the IRS do not permit the inclusion of those amounts in Parts I and II of Form 990 or Form 990-PF or Part I of Form 990-EZ. The optional reporting of donated services and facilities is discussed in the instructions for all three returns.

Amended Returns

If the organization submits supplemental information or files an amended Form 990, 990-EZ, or 990-PF with the IRS, it must also send a copy of the information or amended return to any state with which it filed a copy of the return originally to meet that state's filing requirement.

Method Of Accounting

Most states require that all amounts be reported based on the accrual method of accounting.

Time For Filing May Differ
The deadline for filing Form 990, 990-EZ, or 990-PF with the IRS differs from the time for filing reports with some states.

Public Inspection

Form 990, 990-EZ, or 990-PF information made available for public inspection by the IRS may differ from that made available by the state.

- Certain Charitable Contributions – Designated Transactions of Interest Under New Reportable Transaction Regulations

The IRS has issued Notice 2007-72, designating certain transactions as having the potential for tax avoidance or evasion and alerting participants to required disclosures and potential penalties. In these transactions, a taxpayer transfers a membership interest in a limited liability company that directly or indirectly owns real property to a section 501(c)(3) charitable organization or government entity, claiming a charitable contribution deduction for an amount significantly higher than the original purchase price paid by the taxpayer to acquire the interest. Charitable organizations that receive property in these transactions after August 14, 2007, are participants in these transactions for the first year in which their tax returns reflect the acquired interest, which is generally the year of receipt of the interest. For that year, the charity must disclose certain information to the IRS required by the reportable transaction regulations or be subject to penalties as described in the notice.

- Comprehensive Non-Profit Articles of Incorporation: (One Example)

ARTICLES OF INCORPORATION
OF
(PUT NAME OF ORGANIZATION HERE)

(a/an (put state here) Nonprofit Corporation)

The undersigned individual 18 years of age or older, acting as incorporator under the (put name of state here) Nonprofit Corporation Act, adopts the following Articles of Incorporation:

Article I

Name of Corporation and Duration

The name of this corporation is (put name of organization here) (hereinafter referred to as the "Corporation") and its duration shall be perpetual.

Article II

Organization of Nonprofit

This Corporation is a nonprofit, mutual benefit corporation, organized under the (put name of a state here) Nonprofit Corporation Act.

Article III

Statement of Purpose

The purposes for which this Corporation is organized are as follows:

(1) The Corporation is formed as a business league, within the meaning of section 501(c)(6) of the United States Internal Revenue Code of 1986, (hereinafter referred to as the "Code") and the (put name of state here) Excise Tax Law of (put number here), as set forth and revised in (put name of state here) Revised Statutes (put number here). All references to the Code contained herein are deemed to include corresponding provisions of any future United States Internal Revenue Law or Regulation.

(2) In furtherance of the purposes set forth in this Article III the Corporation may exercise all the rights and powers conferred on nonprofit mutual benefit corporations under the laws of the State of (put name of state here).

(3) Notwithstanding any of the above statements of purposes and powers, the Corporation shall not engage in any activities or exercise any powers, whether express or implied, so as

to disqualify the Corporation from exemption from federal income tax under section 501(a) of the Code by reason of being an organization described in section 50l(c)(6) of the Code and from exemption from (put name of state here) income tax by reason of being an organization described in the (put name of state here) Excise Tax Law of (put number here) and corresponding provisions of any future amendments to said statutes.

Article IV

Registered Office and Agent

The name and address of the initial agent for service of process is:
(put name of person or organization here)

(put address here)

Attn: (put name of person here)

Article V

Incorporator

The name and address of the incorporator is:
(put name of person or organization here) (put address here)

Article VI

Initial Principal Office

Until the principal office of the Corporation has been designated by the Corporation in its annual report, notices may be mailed to the alternate corporate mailing address at:

(put address here)

Attn: (put name of person)

Article VII

Members

The Corporation will not have members.

Article VIII

Dedication and Dissolution

In the event of liquidation, dissolution, termination, or winding up of the Corporation (whether voluntary, involuntary, or by operation of law), the Board of Directors shall, after paying or making provisions for the payment of all of the liabilities of the Corporation, transferal of the property and assets of the Corporation to one or more Qualified Organizations, as defined below, as the Board of Directors shall determine. For purposes of this Article VIII "Qualified Organization" shall mean a corporation or other organization organized and operated exclusively for religious, charitable, educational or other purposes meeting the requirements for exemption provided by (put name of state here) Revised Statute (put number here), as shall at the time qualify either (i) as exempt

from federal income tax under section 501(a) of the Code by reason of being an organization described in section 501(c) of the Code, or (ii) as a corporation or other organization contributions to which are deductible under section 170(c)(1) of the Code. No part of the net earnings of this Corporation shall inure to the benefit of, or be distributable to, its members, directors, officers, or other private persons, except that this Corporation shall be authorized and empowered to pay reasonable compensation for services rendered and to make payments and distributions in furtherance of the purposes set forth in these articles.

Article IX

Limitation of Liability

To the fullest extent not prohibited by the (put name of state here) Nonprofit Corporation Act, as it exists on the date hereof or is hereafter amended, a director and/or officer of the Corporation shall not be liable to the Corporation or its members for any monetary damages for conduct as a director and/or officer. Any amendment to or repeal of the Article IX or amendment to the (put name of state here) Nonprofit Corporation Act shall not adversely affect any right or protection of a director and/or officer of the Corporation for or with respect to any acts or omissions of such director occurring prior to such amendment or repeal. This provision, however, shall not eliminate or limit the liability of a director or officer for:

(1) Any breach of the director's or officer's duty of loyalty to the Corporation or its members;

(2) Acts or omissions not in good faith or which involve intentional misconduct or a knowing violation of law;

(3) Any unlawful distribution;

(4) Any transaction from which the director or officer derived an improper personal benefit; or

(5) Any act or omission in violation of the (put name of state here) Nonprofit Corporation Act.

Article X

Indemnification

To the fullest extent not prohibited by the (put name state here) Nonprofit Corporation Act, as it exists on the date hereof or is hereafter amended, the Corporation:

(1) Shall indemnify any person who is made, or threatened to be made, a party to an action, suit or proceeding, whether civil, criminal, administrative, investigative, or otherwise (including an action, suit or proceeding by or in the right of the Corporation), by reason of the fact that the person is or was a director of the Corporation; and
(2) This Article X shall not be deemed exclusive of any other provisions or insurance for the indemnification of directors, officers, employees, or agents that may be included in any statute, bylaw, agreement, resolution of members or directors or otherwise, both as to action in any official capacity and action in any other capacity while holding office, or while an employee or agent of the Corporation.

IN WITNESS WHEREOF, the undersigned original incorporator has executed these Articles of Incorporation on _____, 20 ___.
(put name of person here), Incorporator

- Life Cycle of a Public Charity Organizing Documents   **(One Example)**
  Draft A – Charter

Article of Incorporation of the undersigned, a majority of whom are citizens of the United States, desiring to form a Non-Profit Corporation under the Non-Profit Corporation Law of _____, do hereby certify:

First: The name of the Corporation shall be _____.

Second: The place in this state where the principal office of the Corporation is to be located is the City of _____,

_____ County.

Third: Said corporation is organized exclusively for charitable, religious, educational, and scientific purposes, including, for such purposes, the making of distributions to organizations that qualify as exempt organizations under section 501(c)(3) of the Internal Revenue Code, or the corresponding section of any future federal tax code.

Fourth: The names and addresses of the persons who are the initial trustees of the corporation are as follows:

Name_____

Address_____

Fifth: No part of the net earnings of the corporation shall inure to the benefit of, or be distributable to its members, trustees, officers, or other private persons, except that the corporation shall be authorized and empowered to pay reasonable compensation for services rendered and to make payments and distributions in furtherance of the purposes set forth in Article Third hereof. No substantial part of the activities of the corporation shall be the carrying on of propaganda, or otherwise attempting to influence legislation, and the corporation shall not participate in, or intervene in (including the publishing or distribution of statements) any political campaign on behalf of or in opposition to any candidate for public office. Notwithstanding any other provision of these articles, the corporation shall not carry on any other activities not permitted to be carried on (a) by a corporation exempt from federal income tax under section 501(c)(3) of the Internal Revenue Code, or the corresponding section of any future federal tax code, or (b) by a corporation, contributions to which are deductible under section 170(c)(2) of the Internal Revenue Code, or the corresponding section of any future federal tax code.

If reference to federal law in articles of incorporation imposes a limitation that is invalid in your state, you may wish to substitute the following for the last sentence of the preceding paragraph: "Notwithstanding any other provision of these articles, this corporation shall not, except to an insubstantial degree, engage in any activities or exercise any powers that are not in furtherance of the purposes of this corporation."

Sixth: Upon the dissolution of the corporation, assets shall be distributed for one or more exempt purposes within the meaning of section 501(c)(3) of the Internal Revenue Code, or the corresponding section of any future federal tax code, or shall be distributed to the federal government, or to a state or local government, for a public purpose. Any such assets not so disposed of shall be disposed of by a Court of Competent Jurisdiction of the county in which the principal office of the corporation is then located, exclusively for such purposes or to such organization or organizations, as said Court shall determine, which are organized and operated exclusively for such purposes.

In witness whereof, we have hereunto subscribed our names this day of

_____20_____

- Charity - Sample Organizing Documents - Declaration of Trust - Draft B - Chart

The _____ Charitable Trust. Declaration of Trust

Made as of the _____ day of _____, 20 _____,

_____, of _____, and

_____, of _____,

Who hereby declare and agree that they have received this day from

_____, as Donor, the sum of Ten Dollars ($10) and that they will hold and manage the same, and any additions to it, in trust, as follows:

First: This trust shall be called "The _____ Charitable Trust.

Second: The trustees may receive and accept property, whether real, personal, or mixed, by way of gift, bequest, or devise, from any person, firm, trust, or corporation, to be held, administered, and disposed of in accordance with and pursuant to the provisions of this Declaration of Trust; but no gift, bequest or devise of any such property shall be received and accepted if it is conditioned or limited in such manner as to require the disposition the income or its principal to any person or organization other than a "charitable organization" or for other than "charitable purposes" within the meaning of such terms as defined in Article Third of this Declaration of Trust, or as shall in the opinion of the trustees, jeopardize the federal income tax exemption of this trust pursuant to section 501(c)(3) of the Internal Revenue Code, or the corresponding section of any future federal tax code.

Third: A. The principal and income of all property received and accepted by the trustees to be administered under this Declaration of Trust shall be held in trust by them, and the trustees may make payments or distributions from income or principal, or both, to or for the use of such charitable organizations, within the meaning of that term as defined in paragraph C, in such amounts and for such charitable purposes of the trust as the trustees shall from time to time select and determine; and the trustees may make payments or distributions from income or principal, or both, directly for such charitable purposes, within the meaning of that term as defined in paragraph D, in such amounts as the trustees shall from time to time select and determine without making use of any other charitable organization. The trustees may also make payments or distributions of all or any part of the income or principal to states, territories, or possessions of the United States, any political subdivision of any of the foregoing, or to the United States or the District of Columbia but only for charitable purposes within the meaning of that term as defined in paragraph D. Income or principal derived from contributions by corporations shall be distributed by the trustees for use solely within the United States or its possessions. No part of the net earnings of this trust shall inure or be payable to or for the benefit of any private shareholder or individual, and no substantial part of the activities of this trust shall be the carrying on of propaganda, or otherwise attempting, to influence legislation. No part of the activities of this trust shall be the participation in, or intervention in (including the publishing or distributing of statements), any political campaign on behalf of or in opposition to any candidate for public office.

B. The trust shall continue forever unless the trustees terminate it and distribute all of the principal and income, which action may be taken by the trustees in their discretion at any time. On such termination, assets shall be distributed for one or more exempt purposes within the meaning of section 501(c)(3) of the Internal Revenue Code, or the corresponding section of any future federal tax code, or shall be distributed to the federal government, or to a state or local government, for a public purpose. The donor authorizes and empowers the trustees to form and organize a nonprofit corporation limited to the uses and purposes provided for in this Declaration of Trust, such corporation to be organized under the laws of any state or under the laws of the United States as may be determined by the trustees; such corporation when organized to have power to administer and control the affairs and property and to carry out the uses, objects, and purposes of this trust. Upon the creation and organization of such corporation, the trustees are authorized and empowered to convey, transfer, and deliver to such corporation all the property and assets to which this trust may be or become entitled. The charter, bylaws, and other provisions for the organization and management of such corporation and its affairs and property shall be such as the trustees shall determine, consistent with the provisions of this paragraph.

C. In this Declaration of Trust and in any amendments to it, references to "charitable organizations" or "charitable organization" mean corporations, trusts, funds, foundations, or community chests created or organized in the United States or in any of its possessions, whether under the laws of the United States, any state or territory, the District of Columbia, or any possession of the United States, organized and operated exclusively for charitable purposes, no part of the net earnings of which insures or is payable to or for the benefit of any private shareholder or individual, and no substantial part of the activities of which is carrying on propaganda, or otherwise attempting to influence legislation, and which do not participate in or intervene in (including the publishing or distributing of statements) any political campaign on behalf of or in opposition to any candidate for public office. It is intended that the organization described in this paragraph C shall be entitled to exemption from federal income tax under section 501(c)(3) of the Internal Revenue Code, or the corresponding section of any future federal tax code.

D. In this Declaration of Trust and in any amendments to it, the term "charitable purposes" shall be limited to and shall include only religious, charitable, scientific, literary, or educational purposes within the meaning of those terms as used in section 501(c)(3) of the Internal Revenue Code, or the corresponding section of any future federal tax code, but only such purposes as also constitute public charitable purposes under the law of trusts of the State of _____.

Fourth: This Declaration of Trust may be amended at any time or times by written instrument or instruments signed and sealed by the trustees, and acknowledged by any of the trustees, provided that no amendment shall authorize the trustees to conduct the affairs of this trust in any manner or for any purpose contrary to the provisions of section 501(c)(3) of the Internal Revenue Code, or the corresponding section of any future federal tax code. An amendment of the provisions of this Article Fourth (or any amendment to it) shall be valid only if and to the extent that such amendment further restricts the trustees' amending power. All instruments amending this Declaration of Trust shall be noted upon or kept attached to the executed original of this Declaration of Trust held by the trustees.

Fifth: Any trustee under this Declaration of Trust may, by written instrument, signed and acknowledged, resign his office. The number of trustees shall be at all times not less than two, and whenever for any reason the number is reduced to one, there shall be, and at any other time there may be, appointed one or more additional trustees. Appointments shall be made by the trustee or trustees for the time in office by written instruments signed and acknowledged. Any succeeding or additional trustee shall, upon his or her acceptance of the office by written instrument signed and acknowledged, have the same powers, rights and duties, and the same title to the trust estate jointly with the surviving or remaining trustee or trustees as if originally appointed. None of the trustees shall be required to furnish any bond or surety. None of them shall be responsible or liable for the acts or omissions of any other of the trustees or of any predecessor or of a custodian, agent, depositary or counsel selected with reasonable care. The one or more trustees, whether original or successor, for the time being in office, shall have full authority to act even though one or more vacancies may exist. A trustee may, by appropriate written instrument, delegate all or any part of his or her powers to another or others of the trustees for such periods and subject to such conditions as such delegating trustee may determine. The trustees serving under this Declaration of Trust are authorized to pay to themselves amounts for reasonable expenses incurred and reasonable compensation for services rendered in the administration of this trust, but in no event shall any trustee who has made a contribution to this trust ever receive any compensation thereafter.

Sixth: In extension and not in limitation of the common law and statutory powers of trustees and other powers granted in this Declaration of Trust, the trustees shall have the following discretionary powers.

a) To invest and reinvest the principal and income of the trust in such property, real, personal, or mixed, and in such manner as they shall deem proper, and from time to time to change investments as they shall deem advisable; to invest in or retain any stocks, shares, bonds, notes, obligations, or personal or real property (including without limitation any interests in or obligations of any corporation, association, business trust, investment trust, common trust fund, or investment company) although some or all of the property so acquired or retained is of a kind or size which but for this express authority would not be considered proper and although all of the trust funds are invested in the securities of one company. No principal or income, however, shall be loaned, directly or indirectly, to any trustee or to anyone else, corporate or otherwise, who has at any time made a contribution to this trust, nor to anyone except on the basis of an adequate interest charge and with adequate security.

b) To sell, lease, or exchange any personal, mixed, or real property, at public auction or by private contract, for such consideration and on such terms as to credit or otherwise, and to make such contracts and enter into such undertakings relating to the trust property, as they consider advisable, whether or not such leases or contracts may extend beyond the duration of the trust.

c) To borrow money for such periods, at such rates of interest, and upon such terms as the trustees consider advisable, and as security for such loans to mortgage or pledge any real or personal property with or without power of sale; to acquire or hold any real or personal property, subject to any mortgage or pledge on or of property acquired or held by this trust.

d) To execute and deliver deeds, assignments, transfers, mortgages, pledges, leases, covenants, contracts, promissory notes, releases, and other instruments, sealed or unsealed, incident to any transaction in which they engage.

e) To vote, to give proxies, to participate in the reorganization, merger or consolidation of any concern, or in the sale, lease, disposition, or distribution of its assets; to join with other security holders in acting through a committee, depositary, voting trustees, or otherwise, and in this connection to delegate authority to such committee, depositary, or trustees and to deposit securities with them or transfer securities to them; to pay assessments levied on securities or to exercise subscription rights in respect of securities.

f) To employ a bank or trust company as custodian of any funds or securities and to delegate to it such powers as they deem appropriate; to hold trust property without indication of fiduciary capacity but only in the name of a registered nominee, provided the trust property is at all times identified as such on the books of the trust; to keep any or all of the trust property or funds in any place or places in the United States of America; to employ clerks, accountants, investment counsel, investment agents, and any special services, and to pay the reasonable compensation and expenses of all such services in addition to the compensation of the trustees.

Seventh: The trustees' powers are exercisable solely in the fiduciary capacity consistent with and in furtherance of the charitable purposes of this trust as specified in Article Third and not otherwise.

Eighth: In this Declaration of Trust and in any amendment to it, references to "trustees" mean the one or more trustees, whether original or successor, for the time being in office.

Ninth: Any person may rely on a copy, certified by a notary public, of the executed original of this Declaration of Trust held by the trustees, and of any of the notations on it and writings attached to it, as fully as he might rely on the original documents themselves. Any such person may rely fully on any statements of fact certified by anyone who appears from such original documents or from such certified copy to be a trustee under this Declaration of Trust. No one dealing with the trustees need inquire concerning the validity of anything the trustees purport to do. No one dealing with the trustees need see to the application of anything paid or transferred to or upon the order of the trustees of the trust.

Tenth: This Declaration of Trust is to be governed in all respects by the laws of the

State of _____,

Trustee _____

Trustee _____

(Source: http://www.irs.gov/charities)

For more examples of IRS information refer to the Appendix at the end of this book.

For complete IRS information refer to the IRS we site: (http://www.irs.gov/charities)

The following is an example of things to consider in creating corporation by laws:

ARTICLE I

SHAREHOLDERS

1.1 Annual Meeting. A meeting of shareholders shall be held each year for the election of directors and for the transaction of any other business.

1.2 Special Meeting. Special meetings of the shareholders, for any purpose or purposes, shall be held when directed by the chair of the board/president/board of directors or at the request of the holders.

1.3 Place of Meeting. The board of directors may designate any place, either within or without the said state, as the place of meeting for.

1.4 Action Without a Meeting. Action required or permitted to be taken at any meeting of the shareholders may be taken without a meeting, without prior notice, and without a vote if the action is taken by the holders of outstanding shares.

1.5 Notice of Meeting. Except in accordance with said state and said statute, written or printed notice stating the place, day, and hour of the meeting and, in the case of a special meeting, the purpose or purposes for which the meeting is called, shall be delivered.

1.6 Waiver of Notice of Meeting. Whenever any notice is required to be given to any shareholder, a waiver in writing signed by the person.

1.7 Fixing of Record Date. In order that the corporation may determine the shareholders entitled to notice of, or to vote at, any meeting of shareholders or any adjournment thereof.

1.8 Shareholders' List. After fixing a record date for a meeting of shareholders, the corporation shall prepare an alphabetical list of the names.

1.9 Voting Per Share. Except as otherwise provided in the articles of incorporation or by said state and said statute, each shareholder is entitled to one vote for each outstanding share held by him or her.

ARTICLE II

BOARD OF DIRECTORS

2.1 General Powers. Except as provided in the articles of incorporation and by said state and said statute, all corporate powers shall be exercised by or under the authority of, and the business and affairs of the corporation shall be managed under the direction of, its board of directors.

2.2 Number, Terms, Classification, and Qualification. The board of directors of the corporation shall consist of.

2.3 Regular Meetings. An annual regular meeting of the board of directors shall be held without notice.

2.4 Special Meetings. Special meetings of the board of directors may be called by the chair of the board, the president, or any two directors.

2.5 Waiver of Notice of Meeting. Notice of a meeting of the board of directors need not be given to any director who signs a written waiver of notice before.

2.6 Quorum. A majority of the number of directors fixed by, or in the manner provided in, these bylaws shall constitute a quorum for the transaction of business.

2.7 Effect of Action. The act of a majority of the directors present at a meeting at which a quorum is present when the vote is taken shall be the act of the board of directors.

2.8 Presumption of Assent. A director of the corporation who is present at a meeting of the board of directors or a committee of the board when corporate action is taken shall be presumed.

2.9 Action Without a Meeting. Any action required or permitted to be taken at a meeting of the board of directors or a committee of it may be taken without a meeting if a consent in writing.

2.10 Meetings by Means of Conference Telephone Call or Similar Electronic Equipment. Members of the board of directors may participate in a meeting of the board by means of a conference telephone call or similar communications equipment if all persons participating in the meeting can hear each other at the same time Participation by such means constitutes presence in person at a meeting.

ARTICLE III

OFFICERS

3.1 Officers. The officers of the corporation shall be a chief executive officer, president.

3.2 Appointment and Term of Office. The officers of the corporation shall be appointed annually by the board of directors.

3.3 Resignation. Any officer of the corporation may resign from his or her respective office or position by delivering notice to the corporation.

3.4 Removal. Any officer of the corporation may be removed from his or her respective office.

3.5 President. The president shall be the chief executive officer of the corporation and shall, subject to the control of the board of directors.

3.6 Compensation. The compensation of the officers of the corporation shall be fixed from time to time by the board of directors.

ARTICLE IV

CERTIFICATES OF STOCK

4.1 Certificates for Shares. The board of directors shall determine whether shares of the corporation shall be uncertificated or certificated.

4.2 Transfer of Shares; Ownership of Shares. Transfers of shares of stock of the corporation shall be made only on the stock transfer books of the corporation, and only after the surrender to the corporation of the certificates representing such shares. Except as provided by said state and said statute.

4.3 Lost Certificates. The corporation shall issue a new stock certificate in the place of any certificate previously issued if the holder of record of the certificate can show proof in affidavit form.

ARTICLE V

ACTIONS WITH RESPECT TO SECURITIES OF OTHER CORPORATIONS

Unless otherwise directed by the board of directors, the president or a designee of the president shall have power to vote and otherwise act on behalf of.

ARTICLE VI

AMENDMENTS

These bylaws may be altered, amended, or repealed, and new bylaws may be adopted, by action of the board of directors.

ARTICLE VII

CORPORATE SEAL

The board of directors shall provide for a corporate seal that shall be circular.

BYLAWS MUST CONFORM TO THE STATE LAW IN WHICH YOU ARE INCORPORATING AND COMPLEMENT YOUR ARTICLES AND BUSINESS GOALS THROUGH CONSULTATION WITH AN ATTORNEY.

- What kind of by-laws do you want to use to set up your non-profit organization? Why?

- What kind of guidelines and procedures do you want to use to set up your non-profit organization? Why?

- What is your non-profit organization's plan to manage the various aspects of the organization?

- What is your non-profit organization's plan going to be for accountability?

- What is your non-profit organization's plan for dealing with any lack of accountability?

- What name do you want your non-profit organization to go by? Why?

- What is your non-profit organization's goal, purpose or objective going to be? Why?

- What is your non-profit organization's plan to accomplish its goal/s?

- What other questions can you come up with to address your personal non-profit organization's needs?

Once you have your articles of incorporation approved by your state you can put your non-profit organization to work. The first thing you will want to do is to appoint a director/s, depending on how you set up your bylaws.

- Directors meet and make decisions collectively as the board of directors, have the authority (and responsibility) to manage and run the nonprofit corporation. Many states allow nonprofits to have just one director, but other states require at least three.

- The next thing you need to do is to hold your first Directors' Meeting.

The purpose of the first meeting of the board of directors is to conduct the initial business of the corporation and take care of other formalities, such as recording the receipt of federal and state tax exemptions.

The directors should first adopt the bylaws and elect officers – state law usually requires a president, secretary, and treasurer, and sometimes a vice president as well. Then, the directors should authorize the newly elected officers to take actions necessary to start the business of the nonprofit – for example, setting up bank accounts and admitting members.

After the meeting is completed, minutes of the meeting should be created and filed in your corporate records book and sealed with the non-profit corporate seal and appropriate signatures as proof of authenticity.

One of the first things you really want to do in creating your articles of incorporation, by-laws and guidelines and procedures is to get involved with a legal service. You don't want to go it alone. Not in just setting up your non-profit organization, but on an ongoing basis.

When you walk into a city council meeting you will always see an attorney sitting next to the city council to advice, clarification of any potential legal issues and to protect the council from doing anything illegally. The same is true with what you are attempting to do with a non-profit organization. The wisest thing you can do is to seek out help from a legal service entity or an attorney that would provide their services as pro-bono or provide the service for free to the non-profit organization. The benefit to the attorney is that he or she can write off his or her time as a tax write-off.

The same is true with finding an accountant to keep proper financial records and accounting. It is a must to keep order, so seek again pro-bono help. Tax advisers are a must, because of your non-profit's status as an organization. You don't want to make any mistakes and lose your tax-exempt status, so seek again pro-bono help.

If you want to go anywhere you really need a great market to pave the way, so seek again for pro-bono help.

With these key players helping you, then you will discover from these individuals their personal interest in wanting to help out, not for money, but because they are excited to be a part of what you are trying to accomplish. These individuals will act as a synergy core group in moving forward with you in a positive and safe way. Exact bylaws, guidelines and procedures will evolve according to your organization's unique needs and the consideration of other key individuals to be involved as specialists will come to light, as you work together in atmosphere of a pro-bono core group.

Refer to the companion book "How to Become TRULY Rich" from The Legacy Journal Collection<> How To Become Truly Successful for further discussion on this matter.

Remember, you can't solve all of the world's problems, but you sure can make a difference.

Being truly wealthy is making a difference in the lives of other people around you.

Being truly wealthy means that you have the time and the means to make a difference in the world and you are doing it.

$$$$$$$$$

**THIS SPACE IS FOR YOUR
FURTHER JOURNAL NOTES ON CHAPTER 8**

Chapter 9

CAN YOU MAKE A DIFFERENCE IN POLITICS?

POLITICAL SERVICE

THE BUREACRATIC RAT RACE!!!

$$$$$$$$$

- Why should you get involved in politics?

- What kind of politician should you be?

A major problem in the history of America politics is bureaucracy. Bureaucracy, meaning too many people making decisions, means it takes forever to bring about change. Thanks to bureaucracy once something becomes law, good luck getting it off the books, if it turns out not to be a good law. It takes forever to get rid of bad laws.

The capitalistic political system has many checks and balances set up to protect the people of its country. The American system is made up of three branches, the Executive Branch, the Legislative Branch and the Judicial Branch. It's a great idea, but again an awful lot of bureaucracy has to take place.

Bureaucracy can be a most disheartening experience to deal with day in and day out if you want to be a politician that wants to make a difference.

Too many politicians hide behind the bureaucratic rat race to protect themselves. "It's not the politician's fault" if something wasn't passed. Problems can always be blamed onto someone else, some committee or the fact that it never made it to be voted on.

Behind all of the hiding, blaming and just hanging out, a new politician has emerged. It appears today that most politicians represent himself or herself first and then maybe the people. It's what the politician thinks is best. He then tries to con or convince his constituents that he knows what's best. It seems that if the politician convinced or at least appeased the people, they could stay elected. That seems to have become the case.

- How did politicians start thinking they were God or some great power?

- Whatever happened to the idea of a politician, in a republic and democratic society, representing the people for the people?

    Politicians are supposed to be the voice, in person, of the people whom they represent. The idea was great one or two hundred years ago, when people had to travel so long, in order to get anywhere. Phones didn't exist, so the only sure way of getting your message was to send a representative in your behalf.

    To be a politician is a great experience that some people just want to have. On a national level, they even get to live in Washington DC. COOL! The pay is probably better than staying home in whatever state they may come from. It is better pay than what most Americans get.

    Complacency and keeping the status quo may be a good game plan if you want to stay around a long time in politics. If a bill doesn't get passed, oh well. Better luck next time. The politician can always say to his constituents that he tried and will try again next time.

    If you're a politician and like the lifestyle of a politician, it becomes a way of life. Who's in any big rush to make any final decision in politics? Yes, they talk the talk and put on a good speech, but when the day is over, they want to come back tomorrow and play the game of politics again.

    The political arena of the America of today better wake up and stop beating around the bush or there won't be a bush to beat around in the future. Politicians need to make decisions that produce action not decisions that produce more indecisions.

    Politicians need to quit representing themselves and find out what their people really want and then do it. Truly represent the people. Quit trying to con the people into something you want, as their politician.

    You would think that America is being taken over by communism with the band of politicians trying to offer everything to the American people. What's going to happen when all of the promises can't be kept? The people will rebel. Forget about going to Iraq to fight. The American soldiers will be fighting a civil war of sorts right here in the good old U.S.A.

It's far past time to make serious changes in the way things are done in America. The system has become way too cumbersome. It must change. Yes, America will feel the pain of change, but it was the easy life that got America where it is today and the only consequence to get out of it will be hard times for the many millions of Americans that have been conned into trusting false campaigns of yester years.

Politicians, whatever you do, don't decide to not decide. Bureaucracy is killing America.

In the fairness of the politicians of today, there are many good-hearted people out there really trying to do some good. It's a big task to run things the way they are in America today. Our hats are off to most of the politicians for even being there.

Politicians, if you really understood the definition of a leader, you would know that it's up to you to lead the way. That doesn't mean sitting in your office either.

Politicians need to start by cutting their fat pay. Cut either your pay to nothing and keep the millions to live off of that are in your current pensions for your service rendered. Or cut your pensions to nothing and serve with frugality, like most Americans will need to do for many years to come.

Either one or both ideas would be a good example for what's ahead for the American people in what they are going to have to go through in order to preserve America for their posterity.

Politicians, I guess the other choice is to continue in the direction America is going, because there just are no other plans out there. The sad thing though is that bureaucracy doesn't work.

There is one other plan to consider for the future. The American people have been living it for so many years that it's just a part of the American way of life and we don't even see it. Debt, does that sound familiar? We don't know how much longer the American people can continue to pay their minimum monthly debt payments.

The same is true with this once great independent nation we call America, the land of the free and the home of the brave, but it can't continue to borrow money from around the world in order to keep its trillions of dollars in debt payments in check.

I think that whether you are wealthy, rich or poor or want to become truly rich or truly wealthy that you get the picture of some of the possible scenarios of what the future might look like in the world.

- What do you want to do in order to make a difference in your future and the future of your posterity?

    o Only you can decide what your future is going to look like and only you can make the difference.

    o Can you rise above the norm in politics and actually put the people you serve ahead of yourself?

    o Can you actually find out what the people want and vote accordingly, whether it's what you want or not?

As a politician, you don't fight anything out in what you think is right or wrong. You leave it to the people you represent to fight it out or in other words let them express their insights and ideas and then let the people vote for what they want you to do on their behalf.

- Can you represent the majority rule and make it known that is all you stand for?

    o Can you do that? Yes or No

        - Can you stick with it 100% of the time? Yes or No
          Why? or Why Not?

If you can do that then please consider helping in the political arenas of your city, county, state or federal governments and any other political opportunities that may be granted you to give of your time, talents and means in doing good in the world you live in. You are the politician that this country is in need of.

There are some people that volunteer or in other words don't need the income, but are in politics for personal reasons. They may have a private agenda that they want to get run through, such as land they own that they want zoned a certain way or water rights changed into their favor, because they own water somewhere else, etc. These are not the politicians that this country is in need of.

Many politicians do it as a living or as a means of an income and that can be a problem. Such politicians don't necessarily care one way or another what happens, just as long as they still have a job at the end of the day. They run a balancing act between self-preservation and serving the people. These are not the politicians that this country is in need of.

Getting involved in politics is a form of volunteering. Actually, the best kind of politician is probably a volunteer politician. They are only there to serve the people, because they want to be there to do what is right for the people they serve.

❖ The following is a personal brief look into a part of my life:

I have privately considered the political arena for myself many times, but never felt compelled to act on it. For one thing, I don't have the answers to everything and don't want to be portrayed as or acting as if I did. I find it to be a real dog-eat-dog arena and don't care to be bashed or to bash back. I'm about what the people I'd represent want and not about what I want or what other politicians want. I'm more of a problem solver and a solution maker. I like to be thorough yet keep things to the point by keeping things reduced and simplified and in a manageable state of workability. I try to work with the big picture in mind while staying within such parameters. As you read my books and consider past chapters on political issues you can see how I feel about politics and the affairs of the world and how I would do things if I were to ever step into that type of arena.

For the United States of America being considered as a free and independent country most politicians aren't independent or free anymore within this country. The legislative system has enslaved politicians. Politicians generally manipulate or are manipulated behind the scenes. With this mindset in politics today there are rarely any true win-wins, but just a bunch of tradeoffs, which counter each other and as a result no one really wins. It's a win-lose or a lose-win game that is played in politics today. It's a give and take system that has evolved.

If I were to go into politics the only thing at this point, I could really accomplish, due to the extreme bureaucratic setting that is plaguing politics, would be to be the voice of the people that elected me to represent them, be it whether I agreed with them or not. At least their voice would be heard with a true voice that would represent their voice. I would promote new bills or laws that the people I represented wanted and not play games with other politicians.

I don't consider myself as a politician, because I'm not of that mind frame. If I were to become a politician my best asset would be the fact that I'm not of the typical politician mind frame and am not owned or controlled by anyone. I don't care to play games with people's lives.

The only area that has ever kept my personal interest in politics is in the area of the federal legislative branches in either a senate or in a congress capacity. Why one of those political venues? Because it is where my most concern in politics has always been.

It's an area that I feel needs help. It's an area that has too many hands in the pot and is nothing more than a bureaucratic nightmare. It's an area that operates on pork barrel mentality where multiple bills are enacted law without standing on their own individual merit. The idea of pooling bills of all types and sizes into one package to be voted on as a whole is not a smart way of governing, nor does it make for a safe country to live in. It can only lead to a country that is out of control and one that has no real bounds. That's why politics is no more than a, you scratch my back and I will scratch your back political arena. It's time to get back to basics with one vote per item. Sure, it is time consuming, but it is the only truly successful way of doing honest business, especially with the assent of technology and its speed and ease in accomplishing many things all at once.

The citizens really don't have a say anymore in politics. However, politics is an area that affects the lives of so many citizens that are depending on these leaders to be honest, trustworthy and supportive of the people. People need to be able to count on their elected officials to do what's right for the people. It's also where I feel like I could make the most difference if I were to ever make such a decision to do something in politics as far as affecting and helping people in that way.

- ❖ **The following is a personal brief look into another part of my life:**

Another political arena I've always privately been intrigued with is the idea of serving as an American Ambassador to another country. It's an appointed position. Since I'm not in the political arena I'm not known by the powers that be and thus would never be considered in the first place, nor have I had any real experience that would justify anyone considering me to such an appointment. If I ever had such an opportunity to serve my country as an ambassador the qualifications that I would bring to the table would be the same qualities that I would bring if I were ever elected as a senator or congressman.

Refer to the companion book "How to Become Truly Rich" from The Legacy Journal Collection<> How To Become Truly Successful for further discussion on this matter.

Remember, you can't solve all of the world's problems, but you sure can make a difference.

Being truly wealthy is making a difference in the lives of other people around you.

Being truly wealthy means that you have the time and the means to make a difference in the world and you are doing it.

$$$$$$$$$

**THIS SPACE IS FOR YOUR
FURTHER JOURNAL NOTES ON CHAPTER 9:**

Chapter 10

DO YOU NEED A BREAK?

MOTIVATION TIME

HOW ARE YOU DOING?

$$$$$$$$$

Now that you have read to this point in this book:

- What does it mean to be poor?

- What does it mean to you to be poor?

- What does it mean to be rich?

- What does mean to you to be rich?

- What does it mean to be truly rich?

- What does it mean to you to be truly rich?

- What does it mean to be wealthy?

- What does it mean to you to be wealthy?

- What does it mean to be truly wealthy?

- What does it mean to you to be truly wealthy?

Regarding these previous question topics, you have answered in this chapter, consider the following questions regarding the same topics:

- What have you actually done in making these changes and/or improvements in your life?

    o You could consider making a list of all of the things you've done to make a difference in your life since you began reading this book.

- What have you actually done in your past before reading this particular book?

    o You could consider making a list of all of the things you've done to make a difference in your life before you begin reading this book.

    o Your list doesn't have to have anything to do with what you've read so far in this book.

    o Consider both economic and charitable things you have done. In this case make two separate categories.

o Now consider making a list of all of the things you've done for yourself in the past. Consider hobbies, trips, recreational, entertainment, self-improvement and anything else you can remember.

o Now consider making a list of all of the things you've done for your family in the past. Consider time spent, places gone to, things you've helped with and anything else you can remember.

- What haven't you done in your past that you wished you had done or would like to have done?

  o Make a list of all of the things you haven't done that you would like to have done in your life. Consider both economic and charitable things. In this case make two separate categories.

- Make a list of all of the things you haven't done that you would like to do for yourself. Consider hobbies, trips, recreational, entertainment, self-improvement and anything else you can think of.

- Make a list of all of the things you haven't done that you would like to do for your family. Consider time spent, places gone to, things you've helped with and anything else you can think of.

- What do all of these things you've done to this point in your life have to do with being truly wealthy?

    o Make a list of all of the things you've done in your life that have to do with being truly wealthy. Consider both economic and charitable things. In this case make two separate categories.

    o Make a list of all of the things you've done for yourself that have to do with being truly wealthy. Consider hobbies, trips, recreational, entertainment and self-improvement and anything else you can remember.

- Make a list of all of the things you've done for your family that have to do with being truly wealthy. Consider time spent, places gone to and things you've helped with and anything else you can remember.

- What haven't you done that you wished you had done or would like to do?

  - Make a list of all of the things you haven't done that you would like to do in your life that have to do with being truly wealthy. Consider both economic and charitable things. In this case make two separate categories.

o Make a list of all of the things you haven't done that you would like to do for yourself that have to do with being truly wealthy. Consider hobbies, trips, recreational, entertainment, self-improvement and anything else you can think of.

o Make a list of all of the things you haven't done that you would like to do with your family that have to do with being truly wealthy. Consider time spent, places gone to, things you've helped with and anything else you can think of.

Now that you have truthfully and honestly answered these questions:

- What do you see in your life that was different in how you lived your life before you started reading this book?

  o Consider, before you started reading this book, if what you did for yourself was more important to you or was it what you did for your family that was more important to you or what you did for other people more important to you or was it a fairly even mix between all three areas of importance to you?

- **What do you see in your life that is different in how you are now living your life since you started reading this book?**

  o Consider, after you started reading this book, if what you are now doing for yourself is more important to you or is it what you are now doing for your family more important to you or what you are now doing for other people more important to you or is it now a fairly even mix between all three areas of importance to you?

➢ **What do you see in your future as for what is most important to you?**

o Consider if what you will be doing for yourself will be more important to you or will it be what you will be doing for your family as being more important to you or what you will be doing for other people as being more important to you or will it be a fairly even mix between all three areas as being more importance to you?

- ✓ Before you go any farther you need to decide what will be most important to you as you look to your future, your family's future, including your posterity and the future of other people that you may have an impact upon depending on what you decide right now.

- ✓ If you aren't sure about what is more important to you, then there is no reason to go on until you decide.

- ✓ If you want to just be wealthy then you can probably stop reading right now and just do what you want, because it probably won't matter what you do.

- ✓ If you aren't sure what you want to do, but would like to continue to see what the truly wealthy are doing then feel free to continue reading this book.

- ✓ If you want to still consider being truly wealthy, then by all means continue reading this book.

- ✓ If you are committed to being truly wealth, then the rest of this book is for you.

> **Appreciate where you have come from in your life!**

> **Be grateful for where you are now at in your life!!**

> **Enjoy where you are now able to go in your life!!!**

Remember, you can't solve all of the world's problems, but you sure can make a difference.

Being truly wealthy is making a difference in the lives of other people around you.

Being truly wealthy means that you have the time and the means to make a difference in the world and you are doing it.

$$$$$$$$

**THIS SPACE IS FOR YOUR
FURTHER JOURNAL NOTES ON CHAPTER 10:**

Chapter 11

WHY SHOULD YOU SET-UP YOUR OWN PRIVATE LENDING COMPANY?

MONEY MAKER

WHY LET THE BANKING INDUSTRY MAKE MONEY OFF OF YOU!!!

$$$$$$$$$

- Remember the chapter on creating or getting involved in a synergizing group? This is another example of what such a group could potentially do.

- You can make money with this venture, however the difference with this is that it also can benefit the people or entities you loan the money to in being able to grow and accomplish something important to them. If you are doing it for that purpose, then it's a good thing you are doing.

- You can be your own bank. You don't call it a bank, but it does the same thing as a bank.

Private lending is where you act like a bank by setting up private loans for various individuals, groups or companies. You charge the entity you are lending to with various interest rates and if you want to you can even charge a set-up fee. You set deadlines when the loan is to be paid in full and/or monthly payments etc. You can have the borrower put up collateral and penalties outlined if the loan isn't paid on time etc.

You can have partners and or investors where you arrange to loan out the investor or partner's money to other entities. You set up guidelines with the individual partners or investors in what the investor's or partner's money can be lent out for, timelines and what the investors or partners want as security from the borrower.

As a private lender, you can decide if you want to lend the money or not. You are the one in control, not someone else. Private lending isn't secured by the federal government, so it is always a risk for any investor, partner or yourself. That is why you want to be picky with whom you lend to and what is used as collateral from the borrower.

Bridge loan lending is for a short period of time. It could be a matter of a few days to a few months. Bridge Loans usually charge a very high interest rate. For example: Anywhere from 25% to 50% and higher. The person or entity borrowing usually has money coming in from one investment or project and in turn going to another investment or project and just needs some money to cover a deadline until their money comes in.

Short term lending typically lasts from a few months up to a year. Short term loans usually charge a higher interest rate than a conventional bank loan and as much as up to double a conventional bank loan interest rate. The person or entity borrowing may need a short-term loan to use in financing buying a real-estate lot to build a home on. Once the home is built the person switches the loan to a conventional mortgage loan and pays off the private lender from the new mortgage loan.

Long term lending lasts for years. Long term loans usually charge just a little more interest than conventional loans. The person or entity borrowing could be using the money to buy a car or maybe to buy some property to keep for a long period of time to possibly develop later on into a subdivision. It could be a long-term loan to even take the place of a mortgage for a person that might not qualify for a traditional bank mortgage loan.

Long term private lending doesn't make as much interest or profit for the lender, but the lender doesn't have to deal with continually re-lending the money out to different individuals or entities.

Short term or bridge loan private lending makes more interest or profit for the lender, but the lender has to do more work to find, meet with, process and verify credit and dependability of continually new individuals or entities to lend to.

Private lending profit basically depends on how much time you want to put into it. The nice thing with private lending is that it makes for a great residual income. Your money is making more money off of your original money, which is lent out every second of every day.

- Is private lending something you would like to consider doing? Yes Or No Why?

Remember, you can't solve all of the world's problems, but you sure can make a difference.

Being truly wealthy is making a difference in the lives of other people around you.

Being truly wealthy means that you have the time and the means to make a difference in the world and you are doing it.

$$$$$$$$$

**THIS SPACE IS FOR YOUR
FURTHER JOURNAL NOTES ON CHAPTER 11:**

Chapter 12

HOW DO YOU SET-UP YOUR OWN **PRIVATE** LENDING COMPANY?

MONEY IN THE BANK

MAKE MORE MONEY OFF OF YOUR OWN MONEY!!!

$$$$$$$$$

Why not set up your own lending company. This type of lending can be set up in many ways.

- Non-Profit Charity

- Trust

- Family Limited Partnership

- S-Corporation

- Corporation

- Limited Liability Company – LLC

- Etc.

There is no particular entity which a person has to use in order to set up their own lending company. It's up to you in how you want to set up your private lending. The main thing is that you do choose some entity in order to protect you. Choose one that works for you and let it be your guide and protection in how and what you do while lending money.

The biggest challenges are in keeping order to all of your private lending. Keep in mind accounting practices and tax guidelines are a must to keep track of. Make sure you use an accountant and tax advisor in making sure you meet all of the IRS requirements and all of the never-ending changes in laws and procedures that continually take place throughout any given year.

Collections are the biggest problem you may encounter, but it can be made easy if you have guidelines and procedures in place and always abide by them. Keep in mind that you aren't the one collecting, but the company is the collection agency. Keep yourself out of it and it won't become personal, even though you may be the company and the collection person, it's still not you personally. You are following guidelines and procedures as outlined and agreed upon and that you are held to and

bound by, just as the person the money is being lent to is held to and bound by to abide by and in all circumstances as prescribed by the guidelines and procedures which you originally set up in the first place.

Make all penalties and consequences clear. No changing the rules mid-stream. If you made a mistake and it's to the advantage of the borrower, the rules still don't change. However, in the future the rules can be changed regarding any future transactions, but not any transactions that are already in place.

Sad to say, but people will try to take advantage of you, even though you are trying to provide a good service on their behalf. Just stick with the rules or let the rules do the talking for you.

Put yourself in a third person position, such as never using your name but the name of the company or in the name of an officer of the company that is over collections or any other item involved in the lending process. If you allow any part of the lending process to become personal, people will try and take advantage of the situation and use it against you or try and use you as a scapegoat.

You may ask yourself why in the world you would want to lend money to any such person as just indicated. It's simple.

1st You don't know how people are going to react after you grant them a loan. What one says and what one does can change at any time and for any reason.

2nd The person you just lent the money to may not know any better and how to act or not act other than how they have been treated in their past.

3rd Ignorance or lack of understanding is quite often a part of a person that is in need of help and is typically only concerned about him or her selves and isn't used to respecting anyone else.

4th By you allowing a person to have a loan from you and that person benefits from the loan and follows through with their responsibility, the end result will be that that person will be better educated and grow in responsibility.

5th Keep in mind that part of the purpose of lending money is to help the person get ahead financially, but more importantly you are giving that person a chance to experience more in him or herself with integrity, responsibility and a great experience in life. Trust and commitment in character and action become more a part of that individual's life.

6th You are modeling to each person you lend money to the same character and ambition you have. Hopefully they will learn from you and in some way and in some time turn around and do the same thing for someone else. You are teaching people by your example how to become truly wealthy as you.

- The following is an example in setting up an LLC in the state I live in:

**ARTICLES OF ORGANIZATION
FOR
(PUT THE NAME OF THE ENTITY HERE), LLC**

A (PUT THE NAME OF THE STATE HERE) LIMITED LIABILITY COMPANY KNOW ALL MEN BY THESE PRESENT:

That the undersigned, as the sole members of the above-named limited liability company come now for the purpose of forming a limited liability company under and by virtue of the laws of the State of (put state name here) and for that purpose hereby certifies as follows:

ARTICLE I

Name and Classification

The name of this limited liability company shall be (put name of entity here), LLC (Hereinafter referred to as the "Company"). The Company shall be classified as a (put name of entity here) Limited Liability Company.

ARTICLE II

Duration of Company

The period of duration is 99 years from the date of filing of these Articles of Organization with the Division of Corporations and Commercial Code of the Department of Commerce of the State of (put state name here), unless the Company is sooner dissolved pursuant to law or the provisions of the Operating Agreement.

ARITCLE III

Purpose

The business purpose and object for which this company is organized shall be to conduct any or all-lawful business for which limited liability companies may be organized pursuant to the (put state name here) Revised Limited Liability Company Act.

ARTICLE IV

Designated Office and Agent

The business address of this company's initial designated office is:

street or PO Box #
city, state zip

The name and address of its registered agent is:

(put the name of the person receiving the mail)

street or PO Box #
city, state zip

The director of the Division of Corporations and Commercial Code of the Department of Commerce of the State of (put state name here) is appointed as the registered agent for service of process if the aforementioned agent or his successor has resigned, the agent's authority has been revoked, or said agent cannot be found or served with the exercise of reasonable diligence.

The registered agent may resign by filing an original and one copy of a signed written notice of resignation with the division. The appointment of the registered agent ends 30 days after the division receives notice of the resignation.

ARTICLE V

Members/Organizers

This company is to be member managed and the name of the initial members/organizers and their respective street addresses are as follows:

person's name
street or PO Box
city, state zip

All rights at any time conferred upon the member/organizer/manager of this limited liability company by these Articles of Organization are granted subject to the provisions of these Articles and the laws of the State of (put name of state here). If a member sells or assigns an interest in the Company, the purchaser or assignee is entitled to all of the financial rights of the selling or assigning member in the Company.

ARTICLE VI

Capital Contributions

The contributions to capital of a member to this limited liability company may consist of cash, property, services rendered, or a promissory note or other binding obligation to contribute cash or property or to perform services.

ARTICLE VII

Operating Agreements

The members of the company shall have the right to enter into an operating agreement to regulate and manage the affairs of the company in any manner not inconsistent with law or these articles. The power to adopt, alter, amend or repeal the Operating Agreement shall be vested in the members.

IN WITNESS WHEREOF, I, the organizers of this limited liability company have here unto set my hand and seal this ___ day of _____, 20__.

MEMBER:

_____
(put member name here)

REGISTERED AGENT:

_____
(put name of person receiving the mail here)

Other examples of more comprehensive LLC structures and set-ups can be found in The Legacy Journal Collection<> How To Become Truly Successful, in the book titled How To Become Truly Rich, by Charles W West.

Remember, you can't solve all of the world's problems, but you sure can make a difference.

Being truly wealthy is making a difference in the lives of other people around you.

Being truly wealthy means that you have the time and the means to make a difference in the world and you are doing it.

$$$$$$$$

**THIS SPACE IS FOR YOUR
FURTHER JOURNAL NOTES ON CHAPTER 12:**

Chapter 13

WHY SHOULD YOU SET-UP YOUR OWN MICRO-LENDING COMPANY?

MICRO BANKING

HELPING-HANDS <> HELPING- HANDS!!!

$$$$$$$$$

- Do you think most poor people want to be poor? Yes or No
  Why? or Why Not?

- How can a poor person get a chance in life?

- Who believes a poor person can make a difference? What do you believe or what do you think?

- What difference would it make if a poor person owned their own business?

- When will a poor person get their chance to rise up and be recognized?

- Where can a poor person go to start their own business?

- Why typically, can't a poor person get a chance?

Only you can answer these questions. Only you can make a difference in how these questions are answered.

- Do you want to make a difference? Yes or No Why?

- How can you make a difference?

- Who can help you make a difference and how can they help you?

- What can you do to make a difference?

- When can you start making a difference?

- Where can you start making a difference?

- Why do you want to make a difference?

Only you can answer these questions. Only you can implement the answers you come up with regarding these questions.

One area most poor people never get a helping hand in is regarding loans. In the case of loaning money to someone that is poor is the fact that the money will usually be gone as soon as it is received, because they don't know how to handle money. Debt or indebtedness is always a part of a poor person's life.

The best way to loan money to a person that doesn't have the means to qualify for a loan is if it is a situation where the loan can enable the person to make money. In time the person pays back what was borrowed in the first place. The best way for this to happen is if the person desiring or seeking a loan has a realistic business venture in place and a plan of action. In most cases like this the person already has some form of a business already in place and working, but just needs the capital to let it actually grow or become truly established. It is a business venture that has already proved that it can and does work.

When lending money to a person that doesn't qualify for a loan through any conventional methods the lender doesn't want the borrower to have a bad experience. The risk factors should be minimal if any at all. This kind of lending is truly about helping someone to have a good experience and the rest will take care of itself.

What is this type of lending called? It is referred to as micro-lending, meaning a small amount with the potential of lots of small loans that could be offered to many people.

Micro loans are typically done by individuals or groups of individuals that care about helping out those that would appreciate a helping hand in the right way. This is a powerful tool in making a difference in the world, one person at a time and at the most basic level of humankind.

The old saying of, "Give a man a fish and you feed him for a day. Teach a man to fish and you feed him for a lifetime." This is truly what micro lending is all about.

True micro lending should be about more than just lending money, but about teaching by example how to manage money and money matters. Not only can you help someone develop a business, but you can also teach better ways to live and improve someone's life. Such a person looks up to you and appreciates and respects you. If you are willing, then such a person is more than likely very willing to trust you as you trusted him or her in the first place.

The exciting thing about micro lending is the fact that the people you are lending money to know that they are a part of a great cause. The cause is to borrow the money and then get it paid back as quickly as possible so that someone else in the same need can have access to the same money to grow and improve their life. These people also know that the little bit of interest they pay for their micro loan will mean that more people will be able to get a chance to get a micro loan too. Such people will feel complete and worthwhile and feel like they too are someone important. It's great that they too can be a part of something great. You will feel great because you made it all happen.

True, you too can make money through micro lending, however the difference with this is that it also can benefit the people or entities you loan the money to in being able to grow and accomplish something important to them. If you are doing it for that purpose, then it's a good thing you are doing. Doing good things for other people is going to come back around to you too. It's just what happens when you are lending money in good and right ways.

In micro lending, you use the same governing principles as you would in private lending. The operations, guidelines and procedures are the same. It's just the purpose that is different. Also, the interest percentages are not about gouging people for major financial profits.

> **Do you have it in you to take a chance on someone that no one else is willing to take a chance on? Yes or No**
> **Why? or Why Not?**

> **Is micro lending something you would like to consider doing? Yes or No Why?**

Remember, you can't solve all of the world's problems, but you sure can make a difference.

Being truly wealthy is making a difference in the lives of other people around you.

Being truly wealthy means that you have the time and the means to make a difference in the world and you are doing it.

$$$$$$$$$

**THIS SPACE IS FOR YOUR
FURTHER JOURNAL NOTES ON CHAPTER 13:**

Chapter 14

HOW DO YOU MANAGE YOUR WEALTH?

PORTFOLIO MANAGEMENT

REDUCE AND SIMPLIFY!!!

$$$$$$$$$

- You need to have a plan of action if you want to know where you are going.

- You need to be able to define financially who you are.

- You need to be able to see where you are in order to determine where you are able to go.

- You need to be able to keep your financial affairs in a written format and as simple as possible.

- Whether you have a large estate or a small estate of financial affairs, you need to keep a record of everything.

- The more you have the more will need to be written.

- Simplicity isn't about the length; it's about categorizing and consistency.

- The smartest thing for you to do is to do something.

- What's your management style look like?

If you want to go anywhere in life you need to have a plan and portfolio management is your foundation. A foundation means you know where you are coming from, that you have a point of reference to turn to for safe direction and if you build on a solid foundation, whatever you do will be solid too.

Your plan of action is your financial foundation in writing, which can be applied to anything you do. Each unique situation may have added branches of your foundation, but the consistency is still there. You want your plan of action to be easy to read, because it is always the same system or method of approach. You are able to quickly find information because it will always be in the same place with no matter what financial projects you are involved in.

Here are some of the money management programs that are out there that you could use:

- For the do-it-yourself person there is a company called "Mvelopes."

- If you don't want to do it yourself then you have a financial planner manage your financial portfolio. Financial planners use companies like "Allbridge" or "Emoney."

These companies don't work directly with the public, but only through an adviser, such as a financial planner, to assist you. What these companies provide are online management programs where you can go online and see what is happening with all of your various financial activities. This service keeps track of everything your money does. It even keeps track of your interest and profit or loss in all of your financial activity. It can even pay your bills for you without you having to think twice about it.

The beauty of such service is that you can check at any time to see how you are actually looking financially, such as pie graphs that will visually show you what your money looks like as far as what areas are being the most successful and what areas aren't. What a powerful tool this could be in helping you decide if you want to do more or less of something. The facts and figures are always at your fingertips wherever you are in the world.

If you don't want to keep track of all of your financial affairs yourself, then consider a financial planner or an accountant to manage your financial portfolio. These professional financial managers already have their own program or have access to all kinds of other programs that take care of tracking you financially. You will want to make sure your tax accountant operates in your behalf with current methods and programs that give you quick and detailed information about your financial portfolio for tax considerations, but more importantly to be able to see how efficient your initiatives or thing you are trying to accomplish are doing. You want to know if your allocations are profitable and efficient or not.

The following are some examples of areas to consider in keeping some type of financial accounting and how you go about doing it. This type of information is important to have, whether you are truly wealthy or not:

- You will want to have a copy of your financial portfolio kept with your various portfolio managers with added instructions also should be kept with such information in case of an emergency. Such places may include in your bank safety deposit box, your portfolio manager's office and your home file. Always have a backup of important information about you and always kept in safe places.
    - If something were to happen to you, your information from one of your locations would always be found and available for whoever was to take

care of your affairs if and when you were no longer able to take care of them yourself. Keeping such a record is helpful for you, but it can also be helpful to other people that are responsible for you.

- o Provide at least the following:

    1. Your financial assets

    2. Your financial liabilities

    3. Your financial tax records

    4. Your journal notes

        a. What you've been doing

        b. What you are doing

        c. What you plan to do

            - How you plan to go about doing it

        d. What problems you've had in the past

        e. What problems you're dealing with at present

        f. What problems you perceive in the future

            - How you plan to deal with potential problems

- You will want to keep a journal, notes and agendas.

    - o It may take time, but it will keep you sane as time goes by and you are trying to remember something, but can't or chances are you won't remember it quite right.

    - o You can sleep easier if you take notes, because you won't have to stay up all night thinking about or trying to remember something that was important and are afraid you might forget by morning to protect yourself you want to have written information that you can rely on to back you up if something is in question.

    - o Always date your notes and list specific first and last names of anyone you are making notes of regarding any decisions, encounters, responsibilities or assignments.

- Also, make note of anyone that was a witness to past transactions, encounters, assignments, decisions or responsibilities.

- Always try to get other people to sign and date any contracts, commitments, agreements, decisions, transactions, assignments or responsibilities.

- Have other people sign and date next to your notes in your journal if you care too.

- Agendas can act as a form of a journal and can be used as an easy way to get other people to sign and date such material to keep everyone straight and as a way to remind any and everyone what they committed to or agreed to.

- Consider the who, what, when, where, why and how to approach to make sure you've covered everything that needs to be said.

- You mostly take notes of any problems and what you did to try and rectify the problems.

- The next reason you take notes is in cases where there might be a problem and what you are doing to head it off.

- Finally, you take notes in case there is something important that you don't want to forget.

- Keep your information updated on a regular basis. Once a week, once a month or once quarterly, you decide what works best for you, but do it. It's good for you to review your information once in a while too and this gives you an excuse. By doing that sometimes you get new ideas that wouldn't otherwise come to you.

➢ Your financial portfolio, tax information and journal notes are important information to have, whether you are trying to be truly wealthy or not.

- Do you want things to come to a stop if and when you are no longer able to take care of them yourself? Yes or No Why?

- Do you want things to continue as you would want them, whether you are there or not? Yes or No Why?

Refer to the companion book "How to Become <u>TRULY</u> Rich" from The Legacy Journal Collection<> How To Become Truly Successful for further discussion on this matter.

Remember, you can't solve all of the world's problems, but you sure can make a difference.

Being truly wealthy is making a difference in the lives of other people around you.

Being truly wealthy means that you have the time and the means to make a difference in the world and you are doing it.

$$$$$$$$$

**THIS SPACE IS FOR YOUR
FURTHER JOURNAL NOTES ON CHAPTER 14:**

Chapter 15

WHY SHOULD THE TRULY WEALTHY PROTECT THEMSELVES?

BE PREPARED

PROTECTION DOESN'T JUST MEAN A BODYGUARD!!!

$$$$$$$$

- If you are wealthy, you are a prime target for those that believe in taking from others in order to gain for themselves.

- Being protected doesn't mean people will not come after you and your wealth, it simply means that you have done all that you can do and you go on living your life.

- If you take charge of yourself and take care of yourself, then you'll be better off for it.

- Being wealthy is more than just about having money and things that you can afford.

- Being prepared for anything is a part of truly being wealthy.

  - What would happen to you in your current situation if a major catastrophe struck your community?

- ➢ If you're wealthy, you have the time to plan and prepare to take care of yourself at all times and in most circumstances.

- ➢ We've learned from history that we'd rather be on the safe side of the equation.

  - How about you, what side of the equation do you want to be on?

- ➢ Be prepared and then it's easier to relax when difficult times come your way. You're still in control.

- ➢ The real benefit of being wealthy is that you are still in control.

- ➢ We wouldn't want to be controlled by someone that is either going to take advantage of us or leave us to burn.

Refer to the companion book "How to Become TRULY Rich" from The Legacy Journal Collection<> How To Become Truly Successful for further discussion on this matter.

Remember, you can't solve all of the world's problems, but you sure can make a difference.

Being truly wealthy is making a difference in the lives of other people around you.

Being truly wealthy means that you have the time and the means to make a difference in the world and you are doing it.

$$$$$$$$$

**THIS SPACE IS FOR YOUR
FURTHER JOURNAL NOTES ON CHAPTER 15:**

Chapter 16

WHY DO YOU WANT TO BE WEALTHY?

TO BECOME TRULY WEALTHY

THERE IS MORE TO LIFE THAN JUST BEING WEALTHY!!!

$$$$$$$$$

- What does the word wealthy mean?

- What does the word truly have to do with being wealthy?

- What does it mean to be truly wealthy?

- What does your legacy look like today?

    - In essence, what do you see and what do other people see in and about you and what you have done and/or have to leave behind and beyond your lifetime?

- What does your legacy sound like today?

    o In essence, what do you have to say and what do other people have to say in and about you and what you have done and/or have to leave behind and beyond your lifetime?

- What does your legacy feel like today?
    - In essence, what do you feel and what do other people feel in and about you and what you have done and/or have to leave behind and beyond your lifetime?

- **How do you want to see your legacy look in the future and/or be left by and/or be remembered for?**

- **How do you want your legacy to sound like in the future and/or be talked about and/or be remembered for?**

- **How do you want your legacy to feel like in the future and/or be felt by and/or be remembered for?**

- Have I said the word **legacy** enough times?

- Have I used the word **legacy** enough times?

- Have I gotten the point across that the word **legacy** is a big deal?

- Have I gotten the point across that the word **legacy** is important?

    ➢ **Only you are in a position to do something about your legacy!**

    ➢ **Only you can do something about your legacy!**

- **What can you do about your legacy?**

- **What are you going to do about legacy?**

All people are in the process of establishing a legacy. It doesn't matter if you are wealthy, rich, poor or in between. Many legacies don't last very long after a person leaves this life. Why? Because those that continue to live are too busy trying to live their own lives out or in reality, they are too busy creating their own legacies. In most cases these legacies are being created without people ever realizing they are even doing it. Keep in mind that each person's individual legacies are going to be had for either good or bad.

There are varying levels of an individual person's legacy, as far as to what an individual can accomplish or leave behind, once the person is gone from this life. A legacy can include many facets of an individual's life. Some people call it good enough to call their posterity their legacy. That is probably the most basic level of an individual person's attempt at creating a legacy. That is also probably the most important legacy any human being can strive for. The way an individual treats other people becomes a part of a person's legacy or what people remember that individual for. The way a person takes care of things is also remembered as a part of a person's legacy. An individual person's personal or valuable things are pasted on as a person's legacy or memory. Some people own property or a home and, in some cases, it has been passed down from generation to generation and is considered a legacy to pass on to future generations.

Most of these types of legacies happen with or without much effort on an individual person's part. For most people a legacy just happens. Such legacies are important, valuable and needed but these are legacies that the individual person didn't really step out of their element to make happen to any real extent. In most cases, most people are not in a position to do much more than the traditional things that most people do to create and make their individual legacies.

Having both the time and the money can give an individual the ability to do more than the traditional things that are done in a person's life and legacy. The ability or opportunity to step out of the box and do something more is the sign of a lasting legacy that can impact multiple people, facets of life and things of this world for a very long time. Such a legacy is only what a truly wealthy person can do. That is where you come in. That is why it is so important that if you are wealthy that you step out of your comfort zone or box and make a difference and that in and of itself can become your long-lasting legacy. The fact that you stepped out, that you did it! **THE COOL THING** is that you will have done it your way and on your own terms or in essence that you took charge of yourself, you made it happen, you made a difference, you had fun while doing it and it was something you wanted to do or that you had the passion to care about and actually do.

It is true that once in a while a poor person, rich person, truly rich person or wealthy person can create a long-lasting legacy, such as what Mother Teresa, did with her efforts to help the abandoned of the India in comforting them and giving them hope. Joseph Smith Jr., from the Church of Jesus Christ of Latter-day Saints, did it with his spiritual visions that brought about the restoration of ancient principles, practices and ways of life, which lead to him being revered as a modern-day Prophet, Seer and

Revelator by tens of millions of people. Martin Luther, from the Catholic Church, did it with his questioning of whether some of the religious practices of his time were man-made ideas, getting away from the original practices of Catholicism, which lead to a new religion being named after him. Muhammad, from the Islamic religion, did it with his visions, which led to him being revered as a prophet by billions of people. Siddhartha Gautama from the Buddhist religion did it with his spiritual nirvana enlightened equality that led to him being declared as Buddha or the Awakened One by billions of people.

All of these individuals and numerous others throughout the ages have left their legacies that have withstood the test of time. There are other people that are remembered for certain events, in which they played a significant role, such as President George W. Bush and the 9-11 terrorist attack that affected the United States of America and its course decisions; President Ronald Reagan and the Berlin Wall coming down; President Richard Nixon and the Vietnam War conflict; President Kennedy and the race to the moon; Bill Gates and the advancement of the personal computer; Sam Walton and the Wal-Mart Super Stores; Neal Armstrong and the first hu an to step on the moon; Martin Luther King Jr. and the "I have a dream!" human rights speech; The Beetles and the beginning of Rock & Roll; Henry Ford and the automobile; The Wright Brothers and the airplane; Thomas Edison and the light bulb, etc.

However, a legacy that is started isn't as important as the fact that it "IS" started. A legacy is sometimes created by the luck of being in the right place and at the right time. It can also be done with hard work, determination and sacrifice. Making a decision in what you want to do for your legacy is the first step in getting your legacy off in the right direction. The more you can be in control of your legacy and its destiny the better chance you have in directing its development and outcome. Every individual person should strive to do their part to create a legacy for themselves. It may involve people, places or things. It depends on your passion, expertise or opportunity and what you can find to do that can make a difference.

> A legacy can be a business you start or started that can benefit other people by providing employment, products or services. That is your legacy or your brand that can carry on with or without you.

> A legacy can be a lending organization that you start or started that can carry on with or without you.

> A legacy can be a service organization that you start or started that can carry on with or without you and it does whatever you want it to.

> A legacy can be a project that you start or started that can carry on with or without you and it does whatever you want it to.

- A legacy can be an educational that you start or started that can carry on with or without you and it does whatever you want it to.

- A legacy can be a way of living organization that you start or started that can carry on with or without you and it does whatever you want it to.

- A legacy can be a foundation or donation organization that you start or started that can carry on with or without you and it does whatever you want it to.

- A legacy can be anything that you start or started that can carry on with or without you and it does whatever you want it to.

There doesn't have to be just one focus or area that makes up an individual person's legacy. In some cases, it may well be one focus or area due to the nature of what you are devoting your time, talents and means toward, however in many cases your passion, interests and scope may be broad in the things you can do. You can create a legacy with multiple facets or areas of your personal passion, interests, expertise, scope, opportunities or needs at the time. Now, I'd say, that if you were to do multiple things as a part of your legacy, then that is maximizing one's potential in time, talents and means! You are definitely not thinking of yourself when putting your paradigm shift to work in this way.

- Whatever way you decide, **PLEASE**:

    Remember the words, **JUST DO IT!!!** and **DO IT!!!**

Remember, you can't solve all of the world's problems, but you sure can make a difference.

Being truly wealthy is making a difference in the lives of other people around you.

Being truly wealthy means that you have the time and the means to make a difference in the world and you are doing it.

$$$$$$$$$

**THIS SPACE IS FOR YOUR
FURTHER JOURNAL NOTES ON CHAPTER 16:**

Chapter 17

WHY DO YOU WANT TO BE TRULY WEALTHY?

LEGACY

LOOK AT THE GOOD THAT YOU HAVE DONE AND CAN DO!!!

$$$$$$$$$

Here is the final thing that you need to understand that makes the difference between being wealthy and being truly wealthy.

LEGACY!!!

Let me repeat it again:

legacy, Legacy, LEGACY, LEGACY!!!, **LEGACY!!!**

Creating a legacy is the end result of being truly wealthy versus just being wealthy. There is a big difference between the two.

To be wealthy is more about you and only you. Your wealth will last beyond your lifetime, but what will happen to it after that? That is an unknown. If you look at the history books your wealth probably won't be too far behind you in your passing. It will probably end up being gobbled up by someone or something else and be gone before you know it.

➢ To be truly wealthy is ultimately all about leaving a legacy.

- **What's your legacy going to be?**

If you have a legacy in place, all of the work you've done to get to this point in your life will not come to an end when you are done with this mortal life.

To be truly wealthy is about you and what you did with your life to help others be successful too. That in and of itself will be a great legacy to leave your posterity and all of those that you have and/or will have affected after you are gone from this life. But there is much more that you can do with your legacy.

All of the many things as outlined in this book and the many other good and great things that you are and will be inspired to create and do, that you set in place and put into motion, will carry on for as long as you meant them to. In many cases, what you are doing now, when done with the 'big picture in mind', will only continue to grow and expand in perpetuating more good than you could have accomplished in your lifetime. Some things you do now could technically go on forever, depending on what it is you wanted to accomplish in your legacy.

How well you plan and put appropriate management and protective guidelines and procedures in place has a lot to do with preserving your legacy.

Legacy, by definition, is what you want to carry on. The term legacy is generally used if and/or when what is carried on continues to grow and expand. In other words, whatever the legacy is has had a great impact on other people and is meant to bless the lives of other people, both in its present status and in its future status as a developing legacy. A true legacy is not a one-time deal. A true legacy acts as a residual, never-ending, on-going, perpetuating, compounding, growing and expanding. A true legacy has its own lifeblood. A true legacy has the ability to sustain itself. A true legacy has its own life, identity, entity and fulfilling purposes. A true legacy is not dependent on anyone or anything else.

When you're affecting the lives of other people, for good, that is a big deal and it in turn affects other people to do the same in return and that is what your legacy will really stand for. You want your legacy to be perpetual, residual, duplicated and ever growing.

The term legacy can be used for negative impact as well, as history can attest too. Be wise in what you choose to do to be remembered by. It will become your brand, your hallmark and your legacy.

> **A legacy is the ability to affect the lives of countless others with whom you will never actually meet in your lifetime, but they will know you.**

- **What do you want to be remembered for?**

- This book has given you some sound advice and ideas to consider in creating and developing your legacy, which is the sign of a truly wealthy person.
    - What is your legacy going to be?
    - Have you decided? Yes or No
    - What is it going to be?

- If you haven't decided, then it's time to decide.
    - Why haven't you decided to decide?

o When will you decide to decide?

- If you haven't set a date to decide, then right now, set a date to decide by.

- At this point, it's not so much what you decide to do, as much as it is that you decided to do something and set a date to actually get started, if you haven't already done something about it.

  o Are you doing it? Yes or No   Why? or Why Not?

- If you have started, are you enjoying what you are doing?
  Yes or No Why?

- If you haven't decided what to do, then make a list of things that are important to you and share them with other people and get their input:

- o Set your goals.

- o Make a plan of action.

- o Have fun while doing it.

➤ You want to make sure your legacy meets the test of time.

- How is your legacy going to play out with your posterity in the annuls of your life history and time spent here on this earth?

- What good have you brought to this earth while you've been here?

- **What good will you leave this earth when you are done and gone from it?**

Your legacy, with or without realizing it, is being created, even as you finish reading this book. The power behind realizing that it is happening right before your very eyes gives you the incentive to accomplish way more than what would have otherwise been accomplished in your lifetime.

Remember, that whatever you do, your legacy isn't really about you. It's about how you helped other people by making the world a better place wherever you are and by whatever means you could. The greatness of a legacy is the fact that you set in motion something that is important to you and both good and worthwhile in making a difference in the lives of other people. The enduring strength of a legacy is in its ability to sustain itself and carry on with or without you. The most important part of your legacy is in modeling or being a true example to your children and future posterity and to anyone else that is both willing and desirous to do the same.

To know that you are in a position to shape the destiny of future generations, to come, is an amazingly overwhelmingly yet delightful and fulfilling thing to experience. Realize that most of the people that will ever walk on this earth are not in the position you are in, regarding being wealthy and the chance to be truly wealthy by being able to leave a truly long-lasting legacy.

- **Take it!**

- **Go for it!!**

- **Do something about it!!!**

- **Be all that you can be!!!!**

- **Make a difference!!!!!**

- **Bless your life!!!!!!**

- **Bless the lives of your family!!!!!!!**

- **Bless the lives of others!!!!!!!!**

- **Bless the lives of your future posterity!!!!!!!!!!**

- **Bless the future lives of many other people to come!!!!!!!!!!!...**

- **What you are doing now is building a lasting legacy!!!!!!!!!!!...**

- **THANK YOU, THANK YOU, THANK YOU!!!!!!!!!!!!!...**

Remember, you can't solve all of the world's problems, but you sure can make a difference.

Being truly wealthy is making a difference in the lives of other people around you.

Being truly wealthy means that you have the time and the means to make a difference in the world and you are doing it.

- ➢ Remember that whatever you do, your legacy isn't really about you. It's about how you helped other people by making the world a better place wherever you are at and by whatever means you had available at the time.

- ➢ The greatness of a legacy is the fact that you set in motion something that is important to you and is both good and worthwhile in making a difference in the lives of other people.

- ➢ The enduring strength of a legacy is in its ability to sustain itself and carry on with or without you.

- ➢ The most important part of your legacy is in modeling or being a true example to your children and future posterity and to anyone else that is both willing and desirous to do the same.

GOOD LUCK!!!!!!!!!!...

$$$$$$$$

**THIS SPACE IS FOR YOUR
FURTHER JOURNAL NOTES ON CHAPTER 17:**

Chapter 18

WHAT'S IT TAKE TO PUT A LEGACY GAME PLAN TOGETHER?

GAME PLAN

WHAT DOES MY GAME PLAN LOOK LIKE?

$$$$$$$$$

The following are some of my own personal scenarios or game plans I have put together for myself, regarding my legacy. These areas are my own personal interests in trying to make a difference in the world around me, for both now and in the future. What will come of these ideas only time will tell. At least you can see some of my own personal interests in things that I have done am doing, would like to do and am attempting to do.

While writing this book, How To Become Truly Wealthy, I have found myself involved in many worthwhile opportunities in how to be able to try and make a difference in the lives of each of my children and grandchildren. I have tried to add more value to my journals for my children and grandchildren by creating business ventures and humanitarian service opportunities that can further expand my ability to connect with each of my children and grandchildren through modern technology and the many interactive means of exploration. I did this, in part, so that this legacy of mine can have added reason to grow and become more a part of their lives in extending and expanding who they are. My intent is for them to see what they too can be, become, do, be a part of and in being able to expand one's horizon or outlook into potential endless opportunities in who they each are and why they are here on earth and what their endless possibilities are and can be.

The following are some of the things I am now involved in or working on, as a part of my legacy/objectives or purposes in life as a result of rewriting my journal notes into The Legacy Journal Collection <> How To Become Truly Successful. Some of these objectives are indirect in my life and some are quite personal to me:

- As for my legacy, I have put together what is called, The Legacy Journal Collection Foundation. The name for the website is, www.thelegacyjournalcollectionfoundation.org The purpose of the foundation organization is multi-facetted and focuses on a myriad of topics in how to become truly successful in trying to do good and worthwhile things in our lives and the world we live in. The solid foundation or basis of the foundation organization is based on the complete masterful library collection set of, The Legacy Journal Collection <> How To Become Truly Successful and from there myriads of other interactions can take place in order to be of help in all aspects of our lives and the world we live in. The foundation organization has the ability to grow and expand, because of its intent in being built on a solid foundation of trying to do good and worthwhile things.

The foundation organization accomplishes much of these ideas through the www.legacyjournalcollectionfoundation.org in being of help to people with its many tools that are in place to assist people. The foundation organization manages:

THE LEGACY JOURNAL COLLECTION
<>
HOW TO BECOME TRULY SUCCESSFUL

or more commonly referred to as:

<<< THE JOURNAL >>>

BY
C. W. WEST

The complete masterful library collection set include: five different series or categories with three sets of volumes in each series. All of these depict different parts of my life and legacy from my experiences, events and expectations in my life.

Objective 1: The www.thelegacyjournalcollectionfoundation.org is to be **a resource to individuals** through educating, learning, growing and expanding in a person's capability, confidence and capacity to step out of their own box in life and experience the world around them in a positive, proactive and productive way.

This can be accomplished through the foundation organization's **Outlook Resources** sponsorship program, which includes educational help, motivational help, how to help and you can do it too help.

- Ten **Outlook Resources** Areas of Focus:

    1. Outlook - Books (Including The Complete: TLJC Library)
    2. Outlook - CD Audios
    3. Outlook - DVD/Videos (Various Presentations)
    4. Outlook - Additional Products & Services (Sponsorship Program)
    5. Outlook - News Letters (Included With Sponsorship Advertising)
    6. Outlook - Forums (Live Online Presentations)
    7. Outlook - Boot-Camps (In Person Seminars)
    8. Outlook - Synergy (Support Groups)
    9. Outlook - Entrepreneurial and/or Employment Opportunities
    10. Outlook - Local, National, International Connections & Outlooks

Objective 2: The www.thelegacyjournalcollectionfoundation.org **Website** is to help the foundation organization to be able to be **proactive in helping people** by meeting the concerns and needs of people in an arena or setting, which is **designed as a place to go to for an individual to be able to**

have a positive interactive interaction that is both supportive and helpful in find whatever tools a person needs or may be looking for.

- **Three Website Areas of Focus:**

    1. The website is able to do online sales & marketing or promoting multiple types of good, worthwhile and beneficial products to people, as well as links to other beneficial products.

    2. The website is able to do online sales & marketing or promoting multiple types of good, worthwhile and beneficial educational programs and services with their various tools, including scheduling boot-camps and seminars to help people, as well as links to other quality educational programs, services and tools.

    3. The website is able to make positive connections with the rest of the world through the outlook resources of newsletters, blogs and forums. All of these interactive interactions connect people in regard to being truly successful and how to go about doing it. It also provides the possibility for the foundation organization to have its followers request other links or areas of concerns, needs and interests that can be added to the website as possible future positive opportunities to promote and be a part of.

Objective 3: The www.thelegacyjournalcollectionfoundation.org is based on multifaceted **intents/goals** in order to have **a clear path** of direction or focus **to be governed by**.

- **Nine Foundation Organization Intents/Goals Areas of Focus:**

    1. The first intent/goal is to first get people to write down their own feelings, thoughts, ideas, desires, hopes, beliefs, ambitions and experiences, etc., like a journal.

    2. The second intent/goal is to get people to continue writing for the rest of their lives about things that are most important to them.

    3. The third intent/goal is to create a reason for people to want to write. In turn, writing will become a habit in the lives of people that wouldn't normally otherwise choose to write. Once people have both a purpose and an added value or reason to write they will more naturally become excited about actually writing.

    4. The fourth intent/goal is all about being a resource, a tool, a guide and an example to those who want help, who want to change and who want to make a difference for good, but don't know how to.

5. The fifth intent/goal is about helping people who want to actually move forward in making a change in their lives by doing something that will actually make a difference in fulfilling their dreams as well as identifying who they are as a person.

6. The sixth intent/goal is to establish an investment foundation or principle of creating a perpetual, (residual funding program) as a part of a humanitarian services project to continually help educate and inspire people with the use of various resources, in finding a purpose to write in particular and a support group as a foundation to help improve that experience for people throughout the world, as a means of expanding a person's potential human capabilities.

7. The seventh intent/goal is to establish a perpetual fund for humanitarian services purposes in part from a perpetual endowment donation of 100%, of all of the proceeds from, The Legacy Journal Collection <> How To Become Truly Successful multi-series.

8. The eighth intent/goal is to establish a non-profit 501(c)(3) organization. **Anyone can be a contributing perpetual endowment sponsor** or make financial sponsorship donations to the organization. This includes any individual person, group, company or entity. All donations are tax deductible and can be donated as an endowment to the organization. All donations go exclusively to meeting the objectives as outlined in the foundation and are protected and secured through legal entities.

9. The ninth intent/goal is for the foundation organization projects to be controlled with progress reports showing all accountabilities and successes.

Objective 4: The www.thelegacyjournalcollectionfoundation.org is meant to act as a **synergy think-tank**. The focus of the synergy think-tank aspect of the foundation organization is intended to be **a catalyst to encourage and help people develop their own legacies**.

- Five **Synergy Think-Tank** Area of Focus:

    1. The first focus is based on helping people with their actual efforts or business venture in things they are doing to get out of debt or becoming truly rich.

    2. The second focus is based on what to do with themselves once they are truly out of debt and wanting to become truly wealthy.

3. The third focus is based on their attitude in life.

4. The fourth focus is based on their gratitude in life.

5. The fifth focus is based on their spiritual or inspirational connections and directions in their life.

Objective 5: The www.thelegacyjournalcollectionfoundation.org is also set-up to operate as an arm of a **humanitarian services foundation**. The humanitarian services foundation has the ability to grow and expand, because of its intent in being built on a solid foundation in trying to do good and worthwhile things in the world we live in.

- **Eight Humanitarian Services Foundation Areas of Focus:**

    1. The humanitarian services foundation or more properly known as the, Perpetual Humanitarian Services Foundation, which operates from or is based on the ability to function from the profits generated from a foundation of never-ending accruing interest money or assets. All donated money or assets are put in holding and can only be used to generate more interest baring funds or profits to operate the humanitarian services foundation programs with their various projects. The funds intent is created to be a vehicle in which people that want to help other people, that are in need, identify those needs and in turn be able to share their time, talents, expertise and know-how with those who are desirous to learn, grow and develop and improve their circumstances in life.

    2. The humanitarian services foundation is **dedicated to people helping people.**

    3. The humanitarian services foundation is focused on **one main goal,** which is to look for opportunities that can potentially change lives for good.

    4. The humanitarian services foundation is all about being **a resource, a tool, a guide and an example** to those who want help, who want to change and who want to make a difference for good, but don't know how to or where to begin.

    5. The humanitarian services foundation is **based on teaching correct principles** to those that might not otherwise know and in turn helping them to learn to govern themselves.

    6. The humanitarian services foundation is established on the

investment foundation or principle of creating a perpetual, **(residual) funding program** to continually do good in the world.

7. The humanitarian services foundation organization is funded, in part, from a **perpetual endowment donation from all of the proceeds/profit generated** from, The Legacy Journal Collection <> How To Become Truly Successful multi-series.

8. The humanitarian services foundation is a **non-profit** 501(c)(3) charitable organization. Anyone can make financial donations to the organization through, The Legacy Journal Collection Foundation as part of one of its programs. All donations are tax deductible and can be donated as an endowment to the organization as a part of the asset perpetual operation to generate accruing interest to operate from. **Anyone can be a contributing perpetual endowment sponsor** or make financial sponsorship donations to the organization. This includes any individual person, group, company or entity. All donations go exclusively to meeting the objectives as outlined in the foundation and are protected and secured through legal entities. All humanitarian service projects are controlled and progress reports are continually posted.

Objective 6: The www.thelegacyjournalcollectionfoundation.org displays the **game**, The Secret Code <> The Treasure Chest Game, which directly involves the players of the game of life in find, opening up and **discovering the many keys that crack open the codes that lead to deciphering all of the many secrets** of life found within the treasure chest. All of, The Legacy Journal Collection <> How To Become Truly Successful secrets are hidden within the contents of the treasure chest and are **there for the discovery for those who are adventurist** in seeking out the truths hidden and waiting therein.

- **Three Secret Code <> The Treasure Chest Game Areas of Focus:**

    1. The game is to get my children interested in reading all of, The Legacy Journal Collection <> How To Become Truly Successful and making it a part of their own lives.

    2. The game is to get grandchildren interested in reading all of, The Legacy Journal Collection <> How To Become Truly Successful and making it a part of their own lives.

    3. The game is to get people interested in reading all of, The Legacy Journal Collection <> How To Become Truly Successful and making it a part of their own lives.

> As for my legacy, let me tell you a little bit about my past in order to understand me a little better in who I am and why some of my areas of interest in the future connect back to my past. One of my accomplishments in life was to retire as a schoolteacher. My retirement from teaching school now provides me with one of my perpetual or residual incomes. The ability to retire from a career is becoming harder and harder, due to the continual movement of people and the lack of job stability in the work force.

As you read, The Legacy Journal Collection <> How To Become Truly Successful, you may see why I write the way I do, because of my background as a teacher, in wanting to involve the participants as much as possible, in order to make what I'm doing what the participants are actually doing too. I like to try to make things as interactive as possible, because to me it's not about me, but rather about the participants and what they may gain from the experience. I like people to participate, to discover on their own and to take ownership in their own learning, because they want to learn, not because they have to learn. Then it will mean something to the learner and will better stay with them. When people can have a real and personal reason to learn, then they will learn that much easier and that much faster, because there is now an added element in the learning process called desire. I like to pose lots of questions and that is a major part of being an educator in creating hypothesis to discover, verify and prove one way or another. I like things to be done in an orderly fashion and that is a very important skill that is continually taught to help students in keeping track of the many and varied things they may find themselves involved in, which in turn become invaluable life skills as well. As a teacher, I tried to emphasize the fact that we are only human beings and can't remember everything, especially in an age of technology where everything continually changes, of course for the better. Right? So, the most important skill to develop is in learning how to use the resources that are available and being willing to search and research or using study skills to help you stay on top of the world versus trying to memorize it all and feel like you are failing by not being able to keep up with it all. As a result, of developing such skills, when you truly need something, you have the skills and the ability to go after it and find it for yourself and put it to work. The good thing with this approach is that you are studied out and ready to go with the most current knowledge and it is all fresh in your mind in what to do versus trying to rely on old information that is mixed in somewhere in your mind along with everything else that is not really fresh in your mind if you were to continually try and rely on such knowledge, which can bring about many mistakes and errors in ones decisions.

While employed as a teacher I worked with over 15,000 students over many years during my educational career. I tried to do my best in making the world a better place for each of the students I worked with. I trust that a part of my legacy or what I tried to share with the students through my example along with the interaction of knowledge between students and teacher is being carried on by the many students I taught over the years. Though our lives may have gone in many directions over the years, since we were together in a class setting, I am still a part of those students as much as they are a part of me.

Many people tried to discourage me from pursuing a career in education, because it is not a high paying career. Education has always been a passion of mine. I always wanted to give back in this way and in particular to the children and rising generations of the future in making the world a better place for them. As for me, I have always felt lucky and most fortunate. I truly appreciate all of those who went before me and taught me along the way of life.

As a result, I am still interested in helping kids and love to volunteer as a substitute, when time permits, in order to be directly involved with the students in trying to be of help to them as they are in the process of forging their lives.

> As for my legacy, I and my beloved wife have been married for many, many, many years and plan to be for the rest of our lives. For us, it's not about how much longer we will be married. Through thick and thin, both good and bad times, we work it out. We change and we adapt, but most importantly we care about the other person enough to somehow always come through okay. If we each lived our marriage for what is in it for ourselves, then it would have ended a long time ago. Marriage isn't so much about me, me, me, but about the opportunity to give, to share and to care, to be of worth, to be somebody and to be someone important to another person that simply cherishes you back. Marriage is about true devotion or commitment in all areas of life. Marriage is a chance to live a truly happy life. True happiness comes from what you can give rather than what you can get. If your marriage is all about what's in it for you, then it's going to be over very quickly.

For me I've been truly blessed with the most wonderful wife, companion, confidante and best friend and as a result I am a much better person than I would have ever been otherwise. She is the real thing. She is always genuinely caring, friendly and most helpful. She has always strived to take good care of herself and I have admired and appreciated that quality in her very much. She truly is a beautiful and classy woman with nobleness, dignity, great character and one worthy of being a queen. I hope for and work toward the best for her.

Our genuine love for one another ennobles our marriage and is the purest legacy that we can pass on to our family. Our love has grown over the years and will continue to grow through the attributes and virtues of respect, kindness, caring, honesty, trust, integrity and loyalty. The organization of our marriage has the ability to grow and expand, because of its intent in being built on a solid foundation in trying to do good and worthwhile things in the world we live in.

- As for my legacy, I and my wife have been and continue to be the co-founders of a Great and Wonderful family. We love our children very much and care about them deeply. Our children are much of what our marriage has been about and will continue to be for the rest of our lives. All of our children are now married and have children of their own. Each of our children has gone in their own directions and individual pursuits in life, but one thing remains constant and will continue to stand above all else and that is that we are a family. No matter where we each live and no matter what we each may do, we are still family and will always be so. Friends and associates may come and go, depending on what each of us are doing or where we may each live, but family never goes away. Family for us is a constant, for good or bad and through thick or thin and will be so as long as we each live.

- As for my legacy, one of the things that my wife and I look forward to the most is getting to be grandparents. We love our grandchildren very much and look forward to all of the times that we can spend with them. We love sharing them with our children and watching each of them grow up in their own unique, special and fun ways. We hope we are good grandparents and hope to always be

    good grandparents and who knows; someday we may get to be great grandparents and have even more fun together as a family. One way or another we will always hope for the best for each of our children and our future posterity.

    Family is what brings us into life and family is how we live our lives and family will always be there one way or another. Our family is the purest legacy that we can pass on from one generation to another. The organization of our family has the ability to grow and expand, because of **its intent in being built on a solid foundation in trying to do good and worthwhile things in the world we live in.**

- As for my legacy, I am most grateful for my connection with God my Eternal Spirit Father and with my elder spirit brother, Jesus the Christ. I am most grateful for all that they stand for and have done for me, both in this existence here in this mortal life and my eternal spirit's growth and opportunities past, present and future.

    My religion and religious affiliations or spiritual connections, commitments and covenants are who I am and what I stand for. Because of this I am able to carry on a true legacy with true meanings, true purposes, true direction and true intents; without having to be confused or fettered by myself or anyone or anything else.

    My legacy, in all its true sense, is the continuation of my Father in Heaven's legacy. So likewise, is Jesus the Christ's legacy a forever continuation of the Father's legacy, purpose, direction and intent. Through His Atonement and His example, He has and is showing and leading the way to all eternal truths, which lead to all things truly good, truly right, truly true, truly possible and truly eternal in all their true nature and true purpose. This knowledge brightens my life and all that I do and stand for in truly knowing Him and who He really is and actually getting to be a part of Him, with Him and one with each other and all that is a part of Him. We each have the common goal of seeking out and fulfilling all things true, good and eternal.

I may not always receive inspiration or revelation directly from Him, but I am able to always feel His inspiration and am able to be directly connected with Him in all that I may think, say and do. The more effort I put into connecting with Him, being like Him and being with Him the closer we are to each other. It is that simple. By so doing this, that is my true legacy.

That is just what Jesus the Christ has shown us how, why and what to do from all of His life examples in how He so chose to live His life here on this earth and how He has always and is and has so lived His life through all time and all eternity. That is exactly what Jesus the Christ/the Only Begotten Son/the Messiah/the Savior of all things and of all of mankind has always so done in seeking out the Father's plan and following the plan of eternal happiness, which includes the plan of salvation and the plan of eternal life for all eternity past, present and future.

- ❖ One of the many great keys to success is continually found throughout the scriptures.

Proverbs 4:7 (in part)

Quote: "….and with all thy getting **get understanding**."

In other words, don't set on your laurels. Get up and do something about it. Be a true believer or seeker of all things true and right. Seek for and live by the truth and more truth will continually come to you.

Proverbs 3: 5-6

Quote: (5) "Trust in the Lord with all thine heart; and lean **not unto thine own understanding**.
(6) In all thy ways acknowledge him and he shall direct thy paths."

Truly trust Him in all things and in all ways come rain, sunshine and in-between, no matter what and no matter what, all will be well.

Alma 32: 21-43

Quote: (21) "And now as I said concerning faith—**faith is not** to have **a perfect knowledge** of things; therefore if ye have faith **ye hope for things which are not seen, which are true**.
(22) And now, behold, I say unto you, and I would that ye should remember, that God is merciful unto all who believe on his name;

therefore he desireth, in the first place, that ye should believe, yea, even on his word.

(23) And now, **he imparteth his word** by angels **unto men**, yea, not only men but **women** also. Now this is not all; little **children** do have words given unto them many times, which confound the wise and the learned.

(24) And now, my beloved brethren, as ye have desired to know of me what ye shall do because ye are afflicted and cast out—now I do not desire that ye should suppose that I mean to judge you only according to that which is true—

(25) For I do not mean that ye all of you have been compelled to humble yourselves; for I verily believe that there are some among you who would humble themselves, let them be in whatsoever circumstances they might.

(26) Now, as I said concerning faith—that it was not a perfect knowledge—even **so it is with my words**. **Ye cannot know of their surety at first**, unto perfection, any more than faith is a perfect knowledge.

(27) But behold, if ye will awake and **arouse your faculties**, even **to an experiment upon my words**, and exercise a particle of faith, yea, even if ye can no more than **desire to believe, let this desire work in you**, even **until ye believe** in a manner that ye can give place for a portion of my words.

(28) Now, we will compare the word unto a seed. Now, if ye **give place, that a seed may be planted in your heart,** behold, if it be a true seed, or a good seed, if ye **do not cast it out** by your unbelief, that ye will resist the Spirit of the Lord, behold, **it will begin to swell** within your breasts; and when you feel these swelling motions, ye will begin to say within yourselves—It must needs be that **this is a good seed**, or that the word is good, for **it beginneth to enlarge my soul**; yea, it beginneth to **enlighten my understanding,** yea, it beginneth to be delicious to me.

(29) Now behold, would not this increase your faith? I say unto you, Yea; nevertheless it hath not grown up to a perfect knowledge.

(30) But behold, as the seed swelleth, and sprouteth, and beginneth to grow, then you must needs say that the seed is good; for behold it swelleth, and sprouteth, and beginneth to grow. And now, behold, will not this strengthen your faith? Yea, it will strengthen your faith: for ye will say I know that this is a good seed; for behold it sprouteth and beginneth to grow.

(31) And now, behold, are ye sure that this **is a good seed?** I say unto you, Yea; for every seed bringeth forth unto its own likeness.

(32) Therefore, **if a seed groweth it is good, but if it groweth not, behold it is not good**, therefore it is cast away.

(33) And now, behold, because ye have tried the experiment, and planted the seed, and it swelleth and sprouteth, and beginneth to grow, ye must needs know that the seed is good.

(34) And now, behold, **is your knowledge perfect?** Yea, **your knowledge is perfect in that thing**, and your faith is dormant; and this because you know, for ye know that the word hath swelled your souls, and ye also know that it hath sprouted up, that your understanding doth begin to be enlightened, and your mind doth begin to expand.

(35) O then, <u>is not this real?</u> I say unto you, **Yea, because it is light**; and **whatsoever is light, is good, because it is discernible**, therefore ye must know that it is good; and now behold, after ye have tasted this light **is your knowledge perfect?**

(36) Behold I say unto you, **Nay**; neither must ye lay aside your faith, for <u>ye have only exercised your faith to plant the seed</u> that ye might try the experiment to know if the seed was good.

(37) And behold, as the tree beginneth to grow, ye will say: Let us **nourish it** <u>with great care, that it may get root, that it may grow up, and bring forth fruit</u> unto us. And now behold, if ye nourish it with much care it will get root, and grow up, and bring forth fruit.

(38) But <u>if ye neglect the tree, and take no thought for its nourishment, behold it will not get any root</u>; and when the heat of the sun cometh and scorcheth it, because it hath no root <u>it withers away</u>, and ye pluck it up and cast it out.

(39) Now, this is not because the seed was not good, neither is it because the fruit thereof would not be desirable; but it is because your ground is barren, and ye will not nourish the tree, **therefore ye cannot have the fruit thereof**.

(40) And thus, **if ye will not nourish the word**, <u>looking forward with an eye of faith to the fruit thereof</u>, **ye can never pluck of the fruit of the tree of life**.

(41) But **if ye will nourish the word**, yea, nourish the tree as it beginneth to grow, **by your faith with great diligence**, and **with patience**, looking forward to the fruit thereof, it shall take root; and behold <u>it shall be a tree springing up unto</u> **everlasting** life.

(42) And <u>because of your</u> **diligence** <u>and your</u> **faith** <u>and your</u> **patience** <u>with the word in nourishing it</u>, that it may take root in you, behold**, by and by ye shall pluck the fruit thereof, which is most precious, which is sweet above all that is sweet**, and **which is white above all that is white**, yea, and **pure above all that is pure**; and ye shall feast upon this fruit even until ye are filled, that ye hunger not, neither shall ye thirst.

(43) <u>Then</u>, my brethren, **ye shall reap the rewards** of your faith, and your diligence, and patience, and long-suffering, waiting for the tree to bring forth fruit unto you."

I have found that if you really want to make a difference in your life and in the lives of others, you simple need to truly put forth <u>ongoing</u> real/true <u>faith</u>, <u>effort</u> or <u>action</u> into truly/true deep <u>study</u>, truly/true connecting <u>prayer</u> and truly/true honest <u>pondering</u> in ways beyond who you are. By doing so, you will truly become and accomplish more than you ever thought possible. I can testify to that fact, because I am living proof thereof in my life.

I am truly the better person for everything. It truly is great to be able to join in with others who have similar desires, hopes and dreams in seeking out, living by and doing good in all honesty, forbearance and goodwill. It truly is great to be able to share all that one has, is and will ever be, in what is worth living for, with anyone and everyone who is willing, even as a mustard seed, by each of us putting forth our own plow and going to work in doing something worthwhile.

That is what being truly wealthy is all about. You need to let your legacy shine forth, just as I need to let my legacy shine forth. As you go forth, just make sure your motivation is driven by and for the right reason.

May we all have the <u>courage</u> to step up to <u>believe</u>/<u>to accept</u> and the courage to have <u>faith</u>/<u>to act</u> in making a difference in the world we all live in, no matter who we are, where we are or what we are doing or able to do. I can do it and so can you.

For all of this I am truly grateful and even more so for being able to be involved with some of my children and grandchildren as time goes by in such legacy projects. That would truly be the icing on the cake. What would be even greater is to see some of my children and grandchildren find inspiration in coming up with their own things they can contribute and do to make a difference in the world. For me my added delight would be in being able to be a part of their development of their own valiant legacies too.

- Now that you have had a glimpse at some of my interests and potential future and how I look at approaching things:

    o **<u>What's your future looking like</u>**
        - **<u>and what are you going to do about it?</u>**

    o What good, noble, worthy and worthwhile things are you going to stand for?

$$$$$$$$$

**THIS SPACE IS FOR YOUR
FURTHER JOURNAL NOTES ON CHAPTER 18:**

Chapter 19

WHAT MIGHT BE SOME OBSTACLES TO WATCH OUT FOR IN BUILDING YOUR LEGACY?

ORCHESTRATING OBSTACLES

OBSTACLES CAN BE TURNED TO BUILDING BLOCKS!

$$$$$$$$$

Now, in the way of being truly wealthy, in building one's legacy worth living for and worth passing on, there are a few things I would like to emphasize as you find yourself potentially interacting and engaging with other people as a part of developing your legacy.

When you are in charge of something or trying to make something happen, such as promoting or trying to move something forward, such as your legacy or whatever it is you are all about or stand for, set clear paramotors. It's good for you and it's good for anyone and everyone else involved with you. Paramotors are what you can live with or accept and work within, however things may go therein and can act as a good or stabilizing guideline. You want to make your paramotors clear to everyone involved so that they know how best to support you in what you are wanting to accomplish.

From there, you need to be a trusting person. Just as you trust yourself, you need to be open and willing to trust other people too. If and when you delegate to other people, which I hope you do all of the time, you need to be willing and open to letting each person run with whatever it is you have asked or put him or her in charge of. Be willing and open to letting each person take charge in whatever way he or she may feel inspired or impressed to go, just as long as it is within the operating permeators you have set forth.

Whatever you ask someone to do may or may not go exactly like you might like it to go or just the way you might do it and that is OK and should be that way. That is what delegating is meant to create, which is an opportunity for someone else to grow and experience doing something good too, which is in part how a legacy is passed on. Just keep in mind that we each are different and thus no one thing ever is going to be exactly the same and that is OK, just as long as the end result is achieved or accomplished.

Whatever you do, don't be a micro manager over someone else. Once you have set the paramotors you need to get out of the way. Don't be telling someone every little thing they are doing right or wrong or simple taking over or cutting someone off or out of the picture, because it's not exactly the way you would have done it. That's not delegating and people will get tired of you indirectly bullying them around or putting them down by hovering around or over them. Remember, it's not about you. It's about getting other people involved and growing and becoming more like what you have become by having their own experiences to go through in their own acts of trial and error. That's true legacy building or passing on who you are and what is important to you.

If someone isn't performing or is out of bounds you do have to step in to coach, but then get back out of the way and let the person take charge and see what happens from there. You may actually be surprised that your particular way or style isn't the only way to accomplish something worthwhile and still come out where you would like it to be.

The best coaching is to get the other person to teach you what it is he or she is trying to do and how he or she plans to go about doing it and why he or she is doing what he or she is doing in the first place. By being a model yourself by setting paramotors and in turn by letting each person model, show, teach or explain something helps him or her in building confidence in leading each person in how to be a winner too. This type of coaching, by letting each person learn how to win and actually winning at whatever he or she is working on, in your behalf, makes for a win-win for everyone involved. To help someone to be able to do something all on their own two feet is a major part of anyone's legacy or in being able to pass something on.

Someone else's way of doing something may not be your way of doing something and that is OK. You need to be willing to go with the flow and in turn let other people take charge and report back to you all of their successes and failures and let them build from there. By doing this you are modeling on other people in how to give and take while working with other people too. This process of giving and taking is what a true legacy is built on or what can make it a never-ending legacy.

Now, when looking at people, when considering how to work with people or what you can and cannot do or what may or may not work, remember, some people are takers and some people are givers. Some people are needy and some people are helpful. Some people care and some people don't care. Some people go around inspiring, uplifting, encouraging and appreciating what other people do and some people go around turning-off or discouraging other people. Some people draw people to want to be around them or to be like them and some people make other people not want to be around them or to avoid them and definitely not wanting to be like them.

Learn to work with anyone and everyone from wherever he or she is coming from and set directions, goals and objectives as a part of your paramotors with each person in what he or she can or cannot do to fit in and build from there. Let each person do the same thing, however they best can. It gets each person to buy in on whatever you are hoping to ultimately accomplish in making a difference in the world as a part of your legacy being passed on. What's cool is that sometimes someone else may be able to expand your legacy to even greater heights you may not have thought off, were able to or capable of on your own.

Now as you consider matters in the relationship of working with other people you have to consider how each person may work with other people and vice-versa. You can't just put people together and expect things to go well. It's like being a schoolteacher with a class full of kids from all walks of life, financial abilities, opportunities and backgrounds, genetic differences, culture and family differences as well as personality and emotional differences.

When you work with people you will find that some people like to take charge while others simply want to be left alone to do their thing. Some wait for direction and some just take the ball and go with it.

Other scenarios to consider include some people's personalities who whine a lot or always have some problem or something wrong. Some people always need help or always ask for help or like to tell other people to do something that they can and well should simply do themselves. Some simply come with a chip on their shoulder or an ax to grind. Some complain almost no matter what and for no real reason at all. It's just who they are or have developed or have become for whatever reasons. Some are like bumps on a log who won't move or move as slowly as possible, for whatever reason, while others need to be slowed down to stay within the paramotors set in order to keep things moving smoothly with everyone else involved. Some like to watch and some like to be watched. Some aren't sure why they are there or just wanting to be there just to be there or come along. Some are harmful and some are helpful. Some people are outwardly kind while others never show any feelings or emotion of gratitude or appreciation, which leaves people not knowing where they are coming from. Some people like to have some fun, while others don't or are constantly fickle or have lots of mood changes. Some people don't care about what someone else may want to do or how someone else sees things or how someone else feels about things while others ask everyone what is on their mind and try to find common ground for all involved. Some people are aggressive and some are tentative or hesitant. Some people are cautious while others put caution to the wind. Some only see one way or one thing and that is all that goes through their mind and in many cases, builds an obsession within them, while others try to see things from many angles and perspectives.

You will find some people like to butt in or take over whatever may be being talked about. It's like they are the authority on anything and everything, whether they are wanted in the conversation or not. Then there are people that listen, but don't listen. After listening they make comments such as, "Ditto" or "Got It" and then they go off and do something totally different or don't do anything at all. Some people are head-setters and tune out everything, which is OK when not working with or around other people. However, when working with or being around such people continually makes it hard to interact with them. It's like you have to interrupt them anytime you want to or need to talk to them.

Some people, be it they are a person in charge or are the leader and in some cases a worker may act the same way, don't want to hear anything or listen to someone else's opinions. Even if a person is only trying to make sincere or helpful suggestions or observations regarding ideas or concerns in trying to be shared. When this happens, in such cases, people tend to try and avoid such people who don't want to listen or only pretend to listen or only listen, because he or she has to listen. Why? The one who is trying to share something tends to find the person who doesn't want to listen or even consider someone else's advice quite often goes out of their way to find reason to think he or she has to get back at such a person for daring to bring up suggestions or appearing to question their authority or at least that tends to be the misperception. Some people tend to get offended over the slightest of things. You never know what it may be. The end result is that other people will tend to try and avoid such a person or avoid certain situation where that person may be around if at all possible.

Some people have allowed themselves to develop or become quite vulgar or crude as they interact with other people and thus offend people to where other people don't want to be around such a person or try to avoid such a person when and where possible. For these people, such conduct or behavior isn't who they are and they don't want anything to do with it, because by being there or around it; it is as though the offending person is representing them too, as though that is how that person is too or they are condoning such verbiage or conduct as acceptable or all right. In turn, the offender thinks the offended person is the rude one for not allowing them to be who they are or accepting their crudeness as their right to talk and act in such demeaning ways. For the offender, they think it is their right or freedom to be that way, even though they are walking all over someone else's rights or freedoms to do so. There is no such right or freedom to walk all over someone else or force your degrading habits on or around someone else.

All of these people and their peculiarities have a dramatic effect on what can and can't be don't or just how well some things can be done. Their impact can and most likely will be felt for some time. Such scenarios can be ignored, but the truth of the matter will inevitably rear its head. It's best to try to be ahead of the game as much as possible.

These are some of the things you have to consider when interacting with other people and where best to go from there. You don't want certain people together, including yourself. Even though some people may be good at whatever they bring to the table, but in certain situations they may offend, hurt, turn off, make reluctant or discourage other people in what they would otherwise bring to the table or their potential and in some cases, turn people off from wanting to be around them.

You also have to keep these same obstacles in mind when considering projects or actual things you are doing for someone else as an act of service or whatever the reason may be. Even if what you are offering someone as an act of charity, kindness, goodwill or of free service you never really know how someone will take to it, what he or she is actually thinking or how receptive a person will actually be. Everyone will take to what you have to offer in different ways and for various reasons. Some people will whole heartedly want your services while others will fight against it or have nothing to do with It, no matter what it is you have to offer.

When approaching any project, it needs to always be done as a process of give and take and adjustments regarding both those who are providing the service along with those who are the recipients of the service as you attempt to understand who you are actually dealing with and how they might perceive each other. You need to look at who is interacting with whom at any given time and in any given circumstance. This process includes both recipients and those providing service in how they might each affect or come across to one another. The more you can get the recipient to buy in on whatever it is you are doing or have to offer and the more the provider is helpful, friendly and caring the easier it will be for a project to take hold and actually come to fruition.

Most importantly you have to always look at yourself and evaluate yourself, in these different categories or potential obstacles. You will want to know where your personality and abilities will best fit in or understand how you may affect or come across to different types of people.

When working with someone on a project, you don't just drop the person in the middle of it all. You will want to at least try not to do that to someone if you can help it at all.

Sometimes you will find it may not be comfortable working with someone or things may not be going all that well. In these cases, you need to keep in mind that if you invited someone to participate with you, hopefully you had done your due diligence beforehand to try to avoid as many potential problems as possible, but that doesn't mean something will show up later on. In such situations, you at least do your best to make it work as well as you can. At a later time, after the project is done, when considering future projects, the person in question is simply not considered again, for whatever the reason may be. Everyone simply moves on when a project is done.

When trying to do a project, though good, in some cases it just won't work with some people and thus you end up not being able to do the project or at least at a particular time, at a particular place or in a particular situation. So many variables need to be considered and weighed out to actually make things work right or come together. Sometimes a project just won't come together, but the attempt was at least made and that is what is most important. If you don't try to make a project happen, you will never know where you stand.

The end result, when considering your legacy, there is more to it than just saying this is me and this is what I want done, what I am going to do or stand for. It's like an orchestra in getting things to come together and making something beautiful. It takes time and it takes practice, along with a lot of trial and error to make something workable, worthwhile and worth living for.

For some of you, you may be someone that won't have to deal with people very much. That can truly be a relief for some of you. Your interests may be more along the line of quieter or behind the scenes kind of a legacy that you are building on. For example, you may be into art or music. You may be someone that does things with animals or with plant life and its myriads of types of things and places. You may be into oceanography or into extra-terrestrial planets and space. You may be into the field of medicine, chemistry, engineering, etc. Each of these areas of interest come with its own challenges and need to be clarified and paramotors set with whatever your passions may be.

Once there is understanding put into place in seeing the bigger picture of something, not only in your field of interest, but in how it interacts with other fields and other people can open one's eyes to even greater insights. It can help you better see and head off many unforeseen obstacles along the way or at least minimize such challenges and in many cases being able to turn such challenges or obstacles into something positive that you can work with or use or at least know better how to work around or with such obstacles.

$$$$$$$$$

THIS SPACE IS FOR YOUR
FURTHER JOURNAL NOTES ON CHAPTER 19:

APPENDIX

A. Complete List of Comprehensive Questions For Each Chapter In This Book:

B. Other Books The Author Recommends You Read On Becoming Truly Wealthy Matters:

C. What The Author Wants You To Get Out Of This Book:

D. How The Other Wants You To Read This Book:

E. The Reason Why The Author Wrote This Book:

F. The Complete List Of Books Written By The Author:

G. About The Author:

H. Author's Disclaimer:

COMPLETE LIST OF COMPREHENSIVE QUESTIONS
FOR EACH CHAPTER IN THE BOOK

- You will find every question asked in this book.

- You can create your own questions to go along with this book.

- When you separate questions, which is what is done in this section, from its original context, which otherwise gives purpose, meaning and understanding to each question; can leave some questions vague, confusing and sometimes misunderstood when left on its own. That will be the case with some of the questions in this section, however having all the questions together helps to give an overall appreciation of all the questions as a whole.

- By applying questions in a different setting or use can open other opportunities for greater creativity with various forms of application leading to further learning.

Chapter: 1

1. WHAT DOES IT MEAN TO BE WEALTHY?
2. DOES IT REALLY MATTER IF YOU ARE WEALTHY?
3. What do you want to do, be and become in life?
4. How do you plan to go about or achieve becoming, doing and being what you want to be, do and become in life?
5. Does it really matter what you do, be and become in life? Yes or No Why?
6. Does it really matter if you are wealthy, rich or poor? Yes or No Why?
7. Do you want to be poor or in other words in debt? Yes or No Why?
8. Do you want to be out of debt or in other words rich to where you are free and independent from anyone or anything having any control or say over you? Yes or No Why?
9. Are you out for wealth and riches of things and fame? Yes or No Why?
10. Are you out to be free and independent to come and go as you please? Yes or No Why?
11. How can you get more if you are giving your wealth and riches away?
12. What else would you want to be free for?
13. Are you meant to be free to do nothing with yourself or to be counter-productive or worthless in life? Yes or No Why?
14. What's your choice going to be?

Chapter: 2

1. WHAT DO YOU DO ONCE YOU ARE WEALTHY?
2. What does it mean to be wealthy?
3. What does it mean to be truly wealthy?

Chapter: 3

1. WHAT HAS WEALTH DONE TO THE HUMAN RACE?
2. What does history have to do with being wealthy?
3. What can and do the history books have to say about the past, present and the future when it comes to wealth and wealth building?
4. Where do you fit in with history?
5. In history who were the rich and wealthy in the world and in particular in Europe?
6. Is hope just another deception in appearing to appease the majority of people into thinking that they too are a part of the game of politics, government rule and control?
7. How and why did the wealthy depend on slavery so prominently in history?
8. What caused a major shift in wealth, power and control to take place after the Crusades of Europe?
9. What happened to the wealthy after the Crusades?
10. How did the wealthy try to control the people?
11. Why does history appear to be a little bit of both genuine sincerity and deception?
12. Why were large groups allowed to try and step into the shoes of the wealthy?
13. The question for Old Russia was what political system should take the place of the Rule of the czar and his family?
14. What's the difference between capitalism, communism and socialism?
15. What has happened to America?
16. Where's America headed?
17. What do the history books have to say about where America's been and how it's gotten to where it is today?
18. In other words, where are you headed?
19. Have the people of America become so poor that they can't take care of themselves anymore?
20. What system seems to work for you, if you want to be truly rich or truly wealthy? Communism or Socialism or Capitalism Why?
21. Can all three basic philosophies work together to make a better future? Yes or No Why?
22. What other ideas can you come up with that would be worthy to take forward into The future?
23. Where does a wealthy person fit in the future of mankind and their future history?
24. Where do you fit in the future of mankind and their future history?

Chapter: 4

1. HOW CAN A TRULYWEALTHYPERSONBEALEADER?
2. WHAT DO YOU HAVE TO OFFER OTHER PEOPLE?
3. Do you have what it takes to make a difference?
4. How can you make a difference?
5. How do you teach someone how to behave?
6. How to teach someone how to accept, change or to improve?
7. What do you teach other people?
8. How do you lead other people?

Chapter: 5

1. HOW DOES A TRULY WEALTHY PERSON CREATE SUSTAINABLE SYNERGY?
2. CAN YOU TAKE WHAT'S IN YOUR MIND AND TURN IT INTO REALITY?
3. What does synergize mean or what is its objective?
4. One head is good, but how much better are many heads working together?

Chapter: 6

1. CHARITY, IS IT IN YOU?
2. How did a wealthy person get their means or wealth?
3. What is charity?
4. What is love?
5. What does it mean to be a humanitarian?
6. What does it mean to give service?
7. What does it mean to volunteer?
8. What does it mean to "have heart" or "from the heart?"
9. Do you have love in your heart?
10. Do you have a caring heart?
11. Do you have charity in your heart?
12. Do you have humanitarian feelings in your heart?
13. Do you have feelings of service in your heart?
14. Do you have volunteering feelings in your heart?
15. Which feelings do you have?
16. Which feelings do you want to have? Why?
17. Which feelings are you going to have?
18. Which feelings do you need to work on or improve on in order for you to be truly wealthy? Why?

Chapter: 7

1. WHAT ELSE DO YOU CARE ABOUT?
2. From the list of things that are important to you, can you see any that may be important to other people? Yes or No
3. Do you consider some of these other people wealthy individuals? Yes or No
4. Do you consider some of these other people as poor or in need of a helping hand?
5. Would you consider the following ideas as things that you could contribute in the way of some of your possible talents or expertise that could benefit a humanitarian organization? Yes or No Indicate which ones?
    1. Understanding
        - ✓ Help other people understand what the organization is all about.
        - ✓ Organizations need some form of order in what they are trying to accomplish.
        - ✓ Visual or Written examples and directions are a valuable tool to any organization.

2. Interactive
   - ✓ Help other people by interacting with them so that they understand what the organization is all about.
   - ✓ Organizations need someone to represent them by going out to the public and being the voice of the organization. You could be the Public Relations Person.
   - ✓ Involve other people by being interactive with them. Show other people how they too can do it, just like you are doing it.
3. Survival
   - ✓ Humanitarian organizations, just like any business, need help being able to survive the ups and downs that go along with any venture.
   - ✓ Sometimes it is financial support and other times it is legal issues or a whole myriad of different things that can take down a venture.
4. Quality
   - ✓ Humanitarian services, just like any business venture, needs quality people, products and service.

6. What can you do to help any humanitarian organization survive and thrive?
7. What are you going to do?

Chapter: 8

1. HOW DO YOU SET-UP YOUR OWN NON-PROFIT CHARITY ORGANIZATIONS?
2. WHY SHOULD YOU SET-UP YOUR OWN NON-PROFIT ORGANIZATIONS?
3. What kind of by-laws do you want to use to set up your non-profit organization?
4. What kind of guidelines and procedures do you want use to set-up your non-profit organization? Why?
5. What is your non-profit organization's plan to manage the various aspects of the organization?
6. What is your non-profit organization's plan going to be for accountability?
7. What is your non-profit organization's plan for dealing with any lack of accountability?
8. What name do you want your non-profit organization to go by? Why?
9. What is your non-profit organization's goal, purpose or objective going to be? Why?
10. What is your non-profit organization's plan to accomplish its goal/s?
11. What other questions can you come up with to address your personal non-profit organization's needs?

Chapter: 9

1. CAN YOU MAKE A DIFFERENCE IN POLITICS?
2. Why should you get involved in politics?
3. What kind of politician should you be?

4. How did politicians start thinking they were god or some great power?
5. Whatever happened to the idea of a politician, in a republic and democratic society, representing the people for the people?
6. What do you want to do in order to make a difference in your future and the future of your posterity?
7. Can you rise above the norm in politics and actually put the people you serve ahead of yourself?
8. Can you actually find out what the people want and vote accordingly, whether it's what you want or not?
9. Can you represent the majority rule and make it known that is all you stand for?
10. Can you do that? Yes or No
11. Can you stick with it 100% of the time? Yes or No Why? or Why Not?

Chapter: 10

1. What does it mean to be poor?
2. What does it mean to you to be poor?
3. What does it mean to be rich?
4. What does mean to you to be rich?
5. What does it mean to be truly rich?
6. What does it mean to you to be truly rich?
7. What does it mean to be wealthy?
8. What does it mean to you to be wealthy?
9. What does it mean to be truly wealthy?
10. What does it mean to you to be truly wealthy?
11. What have you actually done in making these improvements in your life?
12. What have you actually done in your past before reading this particular book?
13. What haven't you done that you wished you had done or would like to have done?
14. What do you see in your life that was different in how you lived your life before you started reading this book?
15. Consider, before you started reading this book, if what you did for yourself was more important to you or was it what you did for your family more important to you or what you did for other people more important to you or was it a fairly even mix between all three areas of importance to you?
16. What do you see in your life that is different in how you are now living your life Since you started reading this book?
17. Consider, after you started reading this book, if what you are now doing for yourself is more important to you or is it what you are now doing for your family more important to you or what you are now doing for other people more important to you or is it now a fairly even mix between all three areas of importance to you?
18. What do you see in your future as for what is most important to you?
19. Consider if what you will be doing for yourself will be more important to you or will it be what you will be doing for your family as being more important to you or what you will be doing for other people as being more important to you or will it be a fairly even mix between all three areas as being more importance to you?

Chapter: 11

1. WHY SHOULD YOU SET-UP YOUR OWN PRIVATE LENDING COMPANY?
2. Is private lending something you would like to consider doing? Yes or No Why?

Chapter: 12

1. HOW DO YOU SET-UP YOUR OWN PRIVATE LENDING COMPANY?

Chapter: 13

1. WHY SHOULD YOU SET-UP YOUR OWN MICRO LENDING COMPANY?
2. Do you think most poor people want to be poor? Yes or No Why? or Why Not?
3. How can a poor person get a chance in life?
4. Who believes in a poor person to make a difference?
5. What difference would it make if a poor person owned their own business?
6. When will a poor person get their chance to rise up and be recognized?
7. Where can a poor person go to start their own business?
8. Why typically, can't a poor person get a chance?
9. Do you want to make a difference? Yes or No Why?
10. How can you make a difference and how can they help you?
11. Who can help you make a difference?
12. What can you do to make a difference?
13. When can you start making a difference?
14. Where can you start making a difference?
15. Why do you want to make a difference?
16. Do you have it in you to take a chance on someone that no one else is willing to take a chance on? Yes or No Why? or Why Not?
17. Is micro lending something you would like to consider doing? Yes or No Why?

Chapter: 14

1. HOW DO YOU MANAGE YOUR WEALTH?
2. What's your management style like?
3. Do you want things to come to a stop if and when you were no longer able to take care of them yourself? Yes or No Why?
4. Do you want things to continue as you would want them, whether you are there or not? Yes or No Why?

Chapter: 15

1. WHY SHOULD THE TRULY WEALTHY PROTECT THEMSELVES?
2. What would happen to you in your current situation if a major catastrophe struck your community?
3. How about you, what side of the equation do you want to be on?

Chapter: 16

1. WHY DO YOU WANT TO BE WEALTHY?
2. What does the word wealthy mean?
3. What does the word truly have to do with being wealthy?
4. What does it mean to be truly wealthy?
5. What does your legacy look like today?
6. In essence, what do you see and what do other people see in and about you and what you have done and/or have to leave behind and beyond your lifetime?
7. What does your legacy sound like today?
    - In essence, what do you have to say and what do other people have to say in and about you and what you have done and/or have to leave behind and beyond your lifetime?
8. What does your legacy feel like today?
    - In essence, what do you feel and what do other people feel in and about you and what you have done and/or have to leave behind and beyond your lifetime?
9. How do you want to see your legacy look in the future and/or be left by and/or be remembered for?
10. How do you want your legacy to sound like in the future and/or be talked about and/or be remembered for?
11. How do you want your legacy to feel like in the future and/or be felt by and/or be remembered for?
12. Have I said the word legacy enough times?
13. Have I used the word legacy enough times?
14. Have I gotten the point across that the word legacy is a big deal?
15. Have I gotten the point across that the word legacy is important?
16. What can you do about your legacy?
17. What are you going to do about legacy?

Chapter: 17

1. WHY DO YOU WANT TO BE TRULY WEALTHY?
2. What's your legacy going to be?
3. What do you want to be remembered for?
4. What is your legacy going to be?
5. Have you decided? Yes or No
6. What is it?
7. Why haven't you decided to decide?
8. When will you decide to decide?
9. Are you doing it? Yes or No Why? or Why Not?
10. Are you enjoying what you are doing?
11. If you have started, are you enjoying what you are doing? Yes or No Why?
12. How is your legacy going to play out with your posterity in the annuls of your life history and time spent here on this earth?
13. What good have you brought to this earth while you've been here?
14. What good will you leave this earth when you are done and gone from it?

Chapter: 18

1. WHAT'S IT TAKE TO PUT A LEGACY GAME PLAN TOGETHER?
2. WHAT DOES MY GAME PLAN LOOK LIKE?
3. What's your future looking like and what are you going to do about it?
4. What good, noble, worthy and worthwhile things are you going to stand for?

Appendix: How The Author Wants You To Read This Book

1. First things first, let me ask you some questions. Are you going to read this book just for the heck of it, with no real intent in making a difference in your life or are you going to read this book because you want to get something out of it that will help you in being successful in your life?
2. What do you plan on doing as you read this book?
   1. Nothing:
      a. Just read it
      b. Skim through it
   2. Take notes:
      a. How
      b. When
      c. Where
      d. Why
   3. Continually evaluate yourself:
      a. Compare your past experiences
      b. Look at your present situations
3. Do you want to make a paradigm shift in:
   1. How you think of things?
   2. How you look at things?
   3. How you do things?
4. Do you have a written Financial Portfolio of yourself?   Yes or No
5. If so, what's your purpose in having a financial Portfolio?
6. Do you have an organized plan you follow in keeping your tax
7. Have you ever put together an Operating Agreement? Yes or No
8. Have you ever put together an Articles of Organization? Yes or No
9. Have you ever set up a Stock Investment Account with a broker or bought any stock? Yes or No
10. Have you ever made a real-estate investment? Yes or No
11. Have you ever patented an idea of your own? Yes or No
12. Have you ever had Collectible or rare items? Yes or No
13. Have you ever talked to an employer about tax benefits in controlling when you receive your year-end income according to which tax rate percentage bracket you want to end up in? Yes or No
14. Have you ever put together a Plan of Action, if you are in debt, to get out of debt? Yes or No
15. Have you ever put together a Plan of Action to save money and make your money pay you interest? Yes or No
16. Do you have multiple sources of income? Yes or no

17. Do you stay out of debt by only buying what you can actually pay cash for?
    Yes or No
18. Do you know what it means to be truly out of debt? Yes or No
19. Are you out of debt? Yes or No
20. Are you truly out of debt? Yes or No
21. Do you know what it means to be rich? Yes or No
22. Do you know what it means to be truly rich? Yes or No
23. Are you satisfied with your financial circumstances? Yes or No
24. Do you consider yourself to be an independent and free person? Yes or No
25. Do you consider yourself as living at peace with yourself? Yes or No
26. Do you consider yourself as a person that is doing good in the world you live in?
    Yes or No
27. Do you consider yourself as a quitter? Yes or No
28. Do you consider yourself as someone that never gives up? Yes or No

OTHER BOOKS THE AUTHOR RECOMMENDS YOU READ ON MONEY MATTERS

The author of this book recommends **the importance of reading books** on teenage and gratitude matters.

The following is a list of other good authors to consider when reading about money matters:

- Muhammad Yunus – Creating a World Without Poverty: Social Business and the Future of Capitalism 2008
    - He is the Nobel Peace Prize Winner 2008
    - He is the founder of Grameen Bank

- Patrick Hanlon – Primalbranding 2006
    - He is the founder of Thinktopia, Inc.

- Plato – Republic 360 BC
    - As translated by A. D. Lindsay 1935
    - Published by The Franklin Library 1975
        - The 100 greatest Books Of All Times Collection

The author of this book chose these individual authors because he knows for example:

- Each author teaches correct principles.

- Each author comes from different backgrounds.

- Each author really does care about you and is concerned about your future.

- Each author wants you to have a truly productive, rich, rewarding, safe, abundant, fulfilling and purposeful life.

After you read some of these authors' books you may observe some of the influence they've had on the author of this book and the thoughts and concerns he has for you.

WHAT THE AUTHOR WANTS YOU TO GET OUT OF THIS BOOK

Three Purposes or Objectives:

1. This book was written with **three foundation principles** in mind.

    1. **Why you should** be truly wealthy.

    2. **How to organize yourself** to be truly wealthy.

    3. **How to create your own** Legacy.

        ✓ The first principle is intended to help you identify who you are and where you fit in the scheme of the world of wealth. In particular, to determine if you are going to be wealthy or truly wealthy.

        ✓ The second principle is intended to help you protect yourself and your wealth. Learn what not to do and how to do it properly, legally and ethically, so that you can focus your energy in doing worthwhile things that not only benefit you, but benefit others.

        ✓ The third principle is intended to help you explore and identify specific ways to volunteer and share yourself, your time, your talents and your means with others. To help other people by truly making a difference with your life, your family's life and the lives of countless others.

2. The key word, **"TRULY"** in the title of this book, is intended for the reader to **discover what it really means** to be truly wealth versus just wealthy.

    1. What does it mean to be **truly wealthy**?

    2. What do you do once you realize what it means to be **truly rich wealthy**?

    3. What do you do when you realize **there is more to money than just being wealthy**?

        ✓ The key word, "truly" is a derivative of the word true.

        ✓ Synonyms of the key word, "truly" include: accurately, properly, truthfully, etc.

3. This book is intended to be a **working manual** for you. It's a **hands-on-book**. This book is intended to become **your very own personal journal** as pertaining to the many extensive and varied topics as found within the book plus, anything else you wish to write about.

   1. **Write in it.**

   2. **Brainstorm and write your own notes, thoughts and ideas in it.**

   3. **Put your own ideas to work.**

Ten Goals or Achievement:

The first goal - to this book is to keep it simple with short **profound thoughts**.

The second goal - to this book is to encourage the reader to find **useful thoughts**.

The third goal - to this book is to get the reader to create his own **meaningful thoughts**.

- The hope is to show to the reader how simple yet powerful it is to put their own important thoughts down in writing, in a few words, to refer to in the future.

- If the reader can create his own philosophy along the way, it is so much easier to relate your ideas with someone else's ideas. Who knows, someday you might even find yourself quoting yourself.

The fourth goal - to this book is to get the reader to **live his life according to true principles**.

The fifth goal - to this book is to get the reader to **protect and manage wealth in right ways**.

The sixth goal - to this book is to get the reader to commit to making a change for the good by **recognizing one's potential in making a difference**.

The seventh goal - to this book is to get the reader to take a serious **look at the current status of his legacy**.

- It is hoped that the reader will contemplate his circumstance and consider what he wants to be remembered for and what will continue beyond his life.

The eighth goal - to this book is to get the reader to **establish his own charitable and humanitarian foundations and synergizing organizations**.

The ninth goal - to this book is to get the reader to **involve other wealthy people so that they too can become truly wealthy individuals**.

The tenth goal - to this book is to get the reader to **be able to live his legacy** and enjoy the fruits of his labors while he is alive to enjoy it.

HOW THE AUTHOR WANTS YOU TO READ THIS BOOK

BEFORE YOU READ THIS BOOK

SOME THINGS YOU NEED TO CONSIDER BEFORE YOU READ THIS BOOK

THINK BEFORE YOU ACT!!!

First things first, let me ask you some questions. Are you going to read this book just for the heck of it, with no real intent in making a difference in your life or are you going to read this book because you want to get something out of it that will help you in being successful in your life?

- What do you plan on doing as you read this book?

    1. Nothing:

        a. Just read it

        b. Skim through it

    2. Take notes:

        a. How

        b. When

        c. Where

        d. Why

    3. Continually evaluate yourself:

        a. Compare your past experiences

        b. Look at your present situations

        c. Determine your future directions

- Do you want to make a paradigm shift in:

    1. How you think of things?

    2. How you look at things?

    3. How you do things?

Feel free to take notes as you read this book. If you do, it will make a world of difference in how much you allow the ideas in this book to help you.

Remember, as a reader of this book, to not only learn from me as the author of the book, but more importantly the opportunity to interact with me by the way in which I created the book so that **the book also becomes your own personal journal** by being able to write in this book. I want you to be able to write your own personal feelings, insights, past experiences, hopes and dreams, while plotting your own plans of actions in your own life, pertaining to the many extensive and varied topics, as found within this book and anything else you may feel inspired to write about.

Take the time to answer all of the questions that are posed throughout the book. The questions are intended to be prompts to you, while at the same time I try to answer the many and varied questions that go along with my experiences in life. The power of creating or posing questions gives you direction and specific purpose in your pursuit in understanding yourself and what it is you stand for and want to accomplish, which gives reason for further contemplation and research on your part. The end result of each question and final answer is a clear picture of what you have done with yourself in the past and who you have become.

- Take the time to answer each question as each question comes.

- Answer each question as best as you can.

- Whatever you do don't change what you originally wrote once you wrote it. There is great power in being able to go back and compare yourself with who you were compared to what you have become as well as what you first did or thought to what you later on do and think.

- There is added space provided in each chapter for you to be able to come back later on and revise and/or improve your answers to the questions and anything else as you become more clarified and inspired to do so.

- Keep in mind, as you write in this book, that what you write in it will become your journal or your expressions about who you are and what you have done and/or will do.

- Keep in mind that what you write in this book will become a part of your written legacy about you and your hopes and aspirations to inspire those that will someday read this book as a part of your journal collection about you.

The following is a list of questions to prompt you to evaluate yourself regarding your past, present and future perspectives concerning your financial knowledge and experience. You may not have a clue what some of the questions are even about, but that's okay. We'll find out together as you read this book and learn what each idea means and how you can make it work for you.

1. Do you have a written Financial Portfolio of yourself?   Yes or No   If so, what's your purpose in having a financial Portfolio?

2. Do you have an organized plan you follow in keeping your tax information? Yes or No   If so, what's your purpose in keeping track of your tax information?

3. Have you ever put together an Operating Agreement? Yes or No

4. Have you ever put together an Articles of Organization? Yes or No

5. Have you ever set up a Stock Investment Account with a broker or bought any stock? Yes or No

6. Have you ever made a real-estate investment? Yes or No

7. Have you ever patented an idea of your own? Yes or No

8. Have you ever had Collectible or rare items? Yes or No

9. Have you ever talked to an employer about tax benefits in controlling when you receive your year-end income according to which tax rate percentage bracket you want to end up in? Yes or No

10. Have you ever put together a Plan of Action, if you are in debt, to get out of debt? Yes or No

11. Have you ever put together a Plan of Action to save money and make your money pay you interest? Yes or No

12. Do you have multiple sources of income? Yes or no

13. Do you stay out of debt by only buying what you can actually pay cash for? Yes or No

- Do you know what it means to be truly out of debt? Yes or No

- Are you out of debt? Yes or No

- Are you truly out of debt? Yes or No

- Do you know what it means to be rich? Yes or No

- Do you know what it means to be truly rich? Yes or No

- Are you satisfied with your financial circumstance? Yes or No

- Do you consider yourself to be an independent and free person? Yes or No

- Do you consider yourself as living at peace with yourself? Yes or No

- Do you consider yourself as a person that is doing good in the world you live in? Yes or No

- Do you consider yourself as a quitter? Yes or No

- Do you consider yourself as someone that never gives up? Yes or No

THE REASON WHY THE AUTHOR WROTE THIS BOOK

The books that make up The Legacy Journal Collection <> How To Become Truly Successful or more commonly referred to as <<< THE JOURNAL >>> By C. W. WEST are an expression of my love, concern and care for my children, future posterity and anyone else that wishes to partake of this same love, concern and care.

For me it has been a great honor to take the time to express myself by rewriting my original journal notes into these many books. To be able to express myself in such a way has been both liberating and fulfilling. My hope is that the books are of worth to all who read them. It is a feeling of great accomplishment, especially knowing that it was all done for my children and future posterity.

I hope my children and future posterity's lives and your life, as a reader of these books, will be blessed from this effort to produce these many books in:

<<< **THE JOURNAL** >>>

BY

C. W. WEST

THE LEGACY JOURNAL COLLECTION

<>

HOW TO BECOME TRULY SUCCESSFUL

I hope your effort to read all of the books and apply the good that is found within each of the books will be a blessing in your life and the lives of your posterity. It is hoped that you too will be inspired, in your own way, to do the many things that you would like to accomplish in your lifetime.

- **I trust that you too will want to be TRULY SUCCESSFUL in whatever you choose to do!!!**

- **I know that YOU TOO CAN BE TRULY SUCCESSFUL!!!**

- **I know that YOU TOO WILL BE TRULY SUCCESSFUL!!!**

- **I know that YOU TOO ARE TRULY SUCCESSFUL!!!**

The following is the story behind the creation of this book and The Legacy Journal Collection <> How to Become Truly Successful or more commonly referred to as <<< The Journal >>> By C. W. West along with how the story came about and where the story may be headed.

THIS IS MY STORY

ABOUT WHY THE LEGACY JOURNAL COLLECTION WAS WRITTEN

It happened in the spring of 2006 when my wife requested that she would like all of us, (meaning her, myself and all of our children) to make all of our Christmas gifts instead of buying them for each other for our next Christmas. She felt that by giving early notice everyone had plenty of time to work on coming up with things to make and time to actually do it. **It was going to be a year of Christmas with no store-bought presents.** What a challenge. All of us were so used to just going to the store and buying something. Now we had to actually plan ahead and make whatever each of us came up with if we were going to have any gifts to give each other. The end result was that she hoped our efforts would end up being something a little more personal, thoughtful and meaningful. Most of us did meet the challenge and put some thought, time, effort and interest into what we came up with. I appreciated getting to see the expressions of a more sincere relationship as a family, because of this challenge.

I knew immediately what I wanted to do for my Christmas gift to each of my children. This challenge really got me motivated and going with the idea of how to rewrite my journal notes. My challenge was going to be in how to reorganize all of it into something that would be creative, innovative and different and that would be palatable and inviting enough that my children would actually be tempted to open and read it. I knew it would be a major undertaking to get it all done in a matter of a few months, but I already had all of the infrastructure with my actual journals already in place and done.

My first thought was to create one large book. At the time, I had approximately a thousand pages of journal notes to work with. I was going to title the book: From Rags to Riches – How to Become Truly Successful. I was going to title each chapter as steps or Mini Steps To Becoming Truly Successful. I knew immediately that no one would read a great big biography or novel about me anymore than they would be willing to read all of my journal notes. I figured my kids would think "why should I read a book about my dad? I already know all about him." If I was going to get my children to read any book about me, it had to be done in some different way. I concluded that it had to be done in third person format. I felt like if I wrote it for a different audience, such as a book for the general public, my children might actually be impressed enough to consider reading it. I also knew it had to be an interactive book in some way. More like a working manual in which to write, and make notes. By doing this it would make the books more meaningful and of greater value to the reader.

I concluded that in order to get my children to read my journal notes in a book format it had to be broken into smaller parts and with different points or areas of interest to each of the books. I like to do things in threes, so I broke everything into categories or series with three subcategories or volumes to each series, which at this point amounted to twelve books that I would have to create from my journal notes.

The end result became known as:

<<< THE JOURNAL >>>

The collection was broken up into five categories or series with three subcategories or volumes in each category or series.

1. The first category or series deals with:
   Volumes:

   a. The power behind money matters and business ventures for adults.

   b. The power behind knowing the good you can do in the world.

   c. The power behind money matters and business ventures for kids.

2. The second category or series deals with:
   Volumes:

   a. The power behind being introduced to the truth.
   b. The power behind believing.
   c. The power behind faith.

3. The third category or series deals with:
   Volumes:

   a. The power of attitude for adults.
   b. The power of attitude for teenagers.
   c. The power of attitude for kids.

4. The fourth category or series deals with:
   Volumes:

   a. The power of gratitude for adults.
   b. The power of gratitude for teenagers.
   c. The power of gratitude for kids.

5. The fifth category or series deals with:
   Volumes:

   a. The power of reflection.
      - An epilog to all of the books in The Legacy Journal Collection.
   b. The power of questions.
      - All of the questions found in The Legacy Journal Collection.

    c. The power of writing.
- An open-ended book for random thoughts, ideas, feelings, experiences, future memories, etc. to be shared.

My next thought was what a challenge it was going to be to put together fifteen books, but to me it was all worth it, because to me, my wife and children were all worth it. My other concern regarding wanting to re-do my journal notes was to have something that my future posterity might have an interest in and may benefit from getting to know me, their grandfather or great-grandfather. I wanted to put some financial value to the books. I realized the books had to be written in such a way that each book brought out its own quality, needed content and personal value to a reader and so that a high price could be put on each of the books. I wanted my children and grandchildren to view these books as something that was worth a lot of money and potentially of great value to other people and as a result of great value to them as well.

This journal/book project was intended to be a private part of my legacy, a Christmas gift to my immediate family and future posterity. My intent was to come up with a unique way to get my children interested in wanting to read my extensive journal notes and personal biography. By so doing, hopefully they would not forget me and what I tried to do for them by how I lived my life, how I dealt with triumph and hard times.

Once the first book was given as a Christmas gift to my wife and children, other people became aware of the series collection and wanted to buy and read them too. Several people prompted me to consider sharing the books with other people by publishing the collection of series, because of what they were experiencing, as they read the books, was of great value to them too. Other people felt the books were down-to-earth experiences that anyone could relate with and learn from and as a result be able to turn around and be successful too. Many expressed that my writing was honest, straight forward, to the point and written without guile as an author. **The fact that the books were written to my children made the books more personal and meaningful.** They expressed appreciation, as a reader, to not only learn from me as the author of the books, but more importantly the opportunity to interact by the way I created the books so that the books also became the reader's own personal journal or beginning of their own written legacy by being able to write, in each book, their own personal feelings, insights, past experiences, hopes and dreams.

After all of the effort in putting together these books as a legacy to my children and future posterity, I gave the first of the twelve books to my children as a Christmas gift one year. After checking six months later, all of my children admitted they hadn't read it. Most said they flipped through it, but some said they hadn't opened the book. My first thought was, "How am I going to get them to want to read the book?" My next thought was, "How can I get them to want to open the book and read it for themselves, because they want to, because they want to know what's inside it and not because their dad bugged them to read it?"

- At this point, only time will tell if my efforts as a father, to share with my children a little bit about myself, will ever come to fruition.

<><>

THE COMPLETE LIST OF BOOKS WRITTEN BY THE AUTHOR:
C. W. WEST
THE LEGACY JOURNAL COLLECTION

<><>

HOW TO BECOME TRULY SUCCESSFUL

<><>

<<< THE JOURNAL >>>

The complete journal collection includes fifteen books, which are divided into five independent categories or series with each series containing three independent subcategories or volumes:

$$
THE POWER OF TRULY HAVING FINANCIAL FREEDOM
<><>
THREE VOLUME SERIES
$$

Volume One
How To Become <> TRULY – Rich
Volume Two
How To Become <> TRULY – Wealthy
Volume Three
How To Become A <> TRULY – Rich Kid
or from a parent's point of view, referred to as:
How To Help Your Kids Become <> TRULY – Rich

??
THE POWER OF TRULY HAVING THE KEY
<><>
THREE VOLUME SERIES
??

Volume One
What Does It Mean To <> TRULY – Learn
Volume Two
What Does It Mean To <> TRULY – Believe
Volume Three
What Does It Mean To <> TRULY – Have Faith

AAAAAAAAAAAAAAAAAAAAAAAAAAAAAAAAAAAAAAAAAAAAAAAA
THE POWER OF HAVING A TRULY POSITIVE ATTITUDE
<>
THREE VOLUME SERIES
AAAAAAAAAAAAAAAAAAAAAAAAAAAAAAAAAAAAAAAAAAAAAAAA

Volume One
<u>Attitude <> Just For – Adults</u>
Volume Two
<u>Attitude <> Just For – Teenagers</u>
Volume Three
<u>Attitude <> Just For – Kids</u>

GGGGGGGGGGGGGGGGGGGGGGGGGGGGGGGGGGGGGGGGGGGGGGGG
THE POWER OF HAVING A TRULY GRATEFUL HEART
<>
THREE VOLUME SERIES
GGGGGGGGGGGGGGGGGGGGGGGGGGGGGGGGGGGGGGGGGGGGGGGG

Volume One
<u>Gratitude <> Just For – Adults</u>
Volume Two
<u>Gratitude <> Just For – Teenagers</u>
Volume Three
<u>Gratitude <> Just For – Kids</u>

CCCCCCCCCCCCCCCCCCCCCCCCCCCCCCCCCCCCCCCCCCCC
THE POWER OF FOLLOW-UP
<>
THREE VOLUME SERIES
CCCCCCCCCCCCCCCCCCCCCCCCCCCCCCCCCCCCCCCCCCCC

Volume One
<u>The Power Of Reflection <> The Contemplative – Epilogue</u>
<u>For: "The Legacy Journal Collection"</u>
Volume Two
<u>The Power Of Questions <> The Complete – Questions</u>
<u>For: "The Legacy Journal Collection"</u>
Volume Three
<u>The Power Of Writing <> The Continuation Of – Life</u>
<u>For: "The Legacy Journal Collection"</u>

ABOUT THE AUTHOR

Chuck West was originally from Southern California. He married his high school sweetheart and they raised their family in Southern Utah. They've been married for over forty years and have five wonderful children and are proud grandparents of eighteen grandchildren.

Chuck received two Bachelor degrees, one in Elementary Education and the other in Early Childhood Education, as well as a minor in social studies from Brigham Young University. He received his Master's degree in Elementary Education from Utah State University.

Chuck retired as a teacher after being in the field of education for 35 years. He taught mostly 3rd and 6th grade. He had both the pleasure and the fun of working with over 15,000 students in various capacities during his carrier. Chuck's main areas of personal interest in education were being a world history teacher and a physical education teacher.

As a teacher, Chuck liked to engage each student with thought provoking questions, identifiable practical applications and a setting where each student could have a supportive, encouraging and a positive experience in trying out new things. He liked to encourage research, contemplation and supportive teamwork and sportsmanship. His hope was to build true confidence within each student. His approach in education was to try and be fair, honest and helpful and that is how he has tried to approach everything he does in life. You can see his personal educational passions showing forth in all of his books as he engages with each reader.

As you read each of his books you will see that Chuck has had many experiences in many areas of life. His life experiences are filled with a plethora of genres that he has written about.

This book was first started in 2006. It is a part of a series of books comprising of Chuck's personal journal notes that he has put into various individual book formats, comprising of his personal experiences, thoughts, ideas, desires, hopes and dreams. Each book identifies with who he is, why he is and what he has actually done in how he has come to approach life.

Chuck's objective, over a period of ten years, from 2006 and thereafter, was to present some of his books each year, as a personal Christmas gift, to his children and future posterity. After accomplishing that, what further good can come of the books will truly become endless.

Chuck refers to the collection of books as his legacy. It's something he can pass on to his children and his future posterity as well as to anyone else who has a desire to make a difference in his or her own life and the world around each other. Chuck refers to the collection as:

THE LEGACY JOURNAL COLLECTION
<>
HOW TO BECOME TRULY SUCCESSFUL
BY
C. W. WEST

AUTHOR'S DISCLAIMER

Due to the litigious nature of today's world found with some individuals and entities devious intents, the author is forced to include this disclaimer regarding any potential attacks, criticisms and attempts to suppress or discredit the message found within this book or any attempts to blame the author for someone else's decisions, action or results.

The author of this book is presenting some of his own personal journal notes, experiences and insights to his children and future posterity. The author realizes other people will inevitably read this book too. Any and all individuals who may read any part of this book are still solely responsible for their own conclusions, perceptions, decisions and actions. The content found within this book does not give anyone any license to go out and proclaim any certain method, way or procedure in creating, managing or lending money as well as how to or what to do when assisting anyone else in any charitable way or political stance as described in this book. When all things are considered, an individual should consult professional and legal help regarding their own personal, professional and lifelong purposes, goals and objectives, because no one case is the same and varies according to time, locality and unforeseen circumstances. Nor does it mean the author supports or indorses any particular person, party, place or thing if and when it may be ascribed to within this book. All matters within this book are considered as examples for the reader's consideration in first and foremost getting to know the author as a father, grandfather and as a person.

www.ingramcontent.com/pod-product-compliance
Lightning Source LLC
Chambersburg PA
CBHW060410220526

45465CB00008B/2832